P9-CQE-939

THE
HEMINGWAY
BOOK CLUB
of
KOSOVO

THE

HEMINGWAY

BOOK CLUB

of

KOSOVO

Paula Huntley

JEREMY P. TARCHER/PUTNAM
a member of
Penguin Putnam Inc.

Most Tarcher/Putnam books are available at special quantity discounts for bulk purchase for sales promotions, premiums, fund-raising, and educational needs. Special books or book excerpts also can be created to fit specific needs. For details, write Putnam Special Markets, 375 Hudson Street, New York, NY 10014.

Jeremy P. Tarcher/Putnam
a member of
Penguin Putnam Inc.
375 Hudson Street
New York, NY 10014
www.penguinputnam.com

Library of Congress Cataloging-in-Publication Data

Huntley, Paula.
The Hemingway book club of Kosovo / Paula Huntley.
p.   cm.
ISBN 1-58542-211-8
1. Kosovo (Serbia)—Description and travel.
2. Huntley, Paula—Diaries.   I. Title.
DR2077.H86   2003   2002032104
949.71—dc21

Printed in the United States of America
1   3   5   7   9   10   8   6   4   2

This book is printed on acid-free paper. ∞

BOOK DESIGN BY AMANDA DEWEY

For my husband, Ed Villmoare,
who took us to Kosovo

For my students and members of the
Hemingway Book Club of Kosova,
who taught me so much

For all the people of Kosovo/Kosova
who struggle for peace

And in memory of my beloved father,
Paul Bowlin

All of us feel this from the cradle, and know, in some sense, that all the significant movement we ever take is internal.

PICO IYER

This is an accidental book.

My husband, Ed, and I volunteered to live and work in Kosovo after the war. He joined the effort to create a new legal system for the country while I taught English as a second language. Throughout those eight months, I kept a journal and e-mailed parts of it occasionally to friends and family. When I returned to the U.S. I found that my journal had spread through e-mail and had captured the interest and imagination of many Americans I didn't even know. Soon, to my astonishment, I had a book offer.

This journal tells the stories of the Kosovo Albanians I came to know and love during our months in that country, and in particular the students to whom I taught English. Their stories are poignant, tragic, sometimes harrowing, but always full of courage and hope. As I was talking with friends and students each day in Prishtina, I didn't realize I was interviewing them for a book, and they didn't know our conversations would wind up in print. When the possibility of publishing the journal arose, I was determined first to obtain everyone's permission to share these stories.

So, in the spring of 2002, Ed and I returned to Kosovo and reunited with our new Kosovo "family." In almost every instance I received not only permission, but also enthusiasm and encouragement. A few people, their memories of terror still vivid, were reluctant to have their names associated with their stories. In those cases I have changed names and identifying characteristics.

To tell such personal stories one must have extraordinary justification. My justification—which is also the reason these Kosovo Albanians wanted their stories told—is the hope that somehow the book will help this poor, struggling non-country.

It is also my hope that more of us Americans will become involved with the rest of the world. We need to learn about other people, learn what they think of us, try to understand, even if we don't agree with, their points of view. Everywhere in the world, I believe, from our own backyards to the middle of the Balkans, there exist people whose needs, and whose generous, responsive hearts, offer even the most ordinary Americans—like me—an opportunity to serve, to connect, to expand our capacity for love.

Paula Bowlin Huntley
Bolinas, California
September 2002

A NOTE ABOUT PLACE NAMES
AND SPELLINGS

Everyone writing about Kosovo faces the dilemma of whether to use Albanian or Serbian versions of place names. Most atlases use Serbian names. But because I learned about Kosovo's towns and regions from Kosovo Albanians, I use Albanian place names in my journal. The exception is the name of the country itself, which is spelled Kosova by Albanians, but which I call Kosovo, the Serbian word, because that is the name recognized in the English-speaking world. Ironically, although the name of the book club was "The Hemingway Book Club of Kosova," I felt I had to change this to "Kosovo" for the book title, so as not to confuse my American readers. I am sure the members of the club will understand.

THE
HEMINGWAY
BOOK CLUB
of
KOSOVO

PREFACE

MONDAY, OCTOBER 23, 2000
Prishtina, Kosovo

Last week I found a copy of Hemingway's *The Old Man and the Sea*—probably the only one in the country—and had copies of it made for everyone in the class. It's the right length, the prose is simple enough for the intermediate level, and its story, I think, will resonate with these brave young people. I'll have to be alert for Hemingway's macho, though. God knows this country doesn't need any more macho.

I put together from the web a logo with the name of our club, The Hemingway Book Club of Kosovo, and a wonderful drawing of a marlin. I hand it out today to much admiration, and one reservation they all share: "Teacher, you have spelled it 'Kosovo.' That is wrong. It should be 'Kosova.'" Kosova, with an "a," is the Albanian form of the word, and is a political statement. The U.N. doesn't want "Kosova" used because it connotes independence from Serbia. But this book club belongs to these Albanian students. I will change it to Kosova.

Today I give everyone their books and the first set of "focus questions"—things to think about as they read the first twenty pages. Then, on November 11, a Saturday, those who want can come to our house for the first club meeting. Everyone seems to be excited about it. It is, they say, the first book in English they've owned. For some, it is their first book in any language other than texts they use at school. . . .

∽

WEDNESDAY, AUGUST 23, 2000 *(two months earlier)*
Bolinas, California

In three days we leave for Kosovo, and I am scared. Last night I awoke in the middle of the night and sat bolt upright, panicked. "What in God's name are we *doing?*"

I've had three months to get used to the idea. Ever since I came home from work the first of June to hear Ed say he'd been offered the chance to help build a modern legal system there. "Anywhere but Kosovo!" I protested. In Kosovo, where Slobodan Milosevic's bloody last-ditch effort to hang on to Serbian power in Yugoslavia ended only last year, the wounds are still fresh. Kosovo seemed, quite simply, too hard, too sad. But it is Kosovo that offers the greatest challenge for him, and now, for both of us, it is the plight, the courage of the Kosovars that touches our hearts.

So, despite my months of protest, we are going to Kosovo. I keep telling myself that it won't be the first time I have followed my heart into something new and scary. I met Ed twenty-one years ago on a blind date in Little Rock, Arkansas. Two months later I left my job, my friends and family, and everything I owned to go live with Ed in a funky little town in northern California, as different from Little Rock as any place in America could be. I took a chance and was happy I did. So maybe now . . .

Although Kosovo is Ed's idea, his work that will take us there, I know I must find my own way. I know something of what I hope to gain from the experience: a greater tolerance for ambiguity, a greater respect for differences, some clearer understanding of my own capacity for change, maybe. Am I willing to risk turning my own notions of myself and the world upside down? For this, I suspect, is what I'm getting myself into.

I already think of myself as tolerant, open-minded, respectful. But, from what I've read, life in Kosovo may challenge this smug belief. I may find myself wondering where to draw the line: Should endless generational blood feuds be respected? (The ancient Albanian code of conduct, the Kanun of Lek Dukagjin, which I am reading tonight, specifies that blood can only be wiped out with blood.) Should abuse of women be tolerated because it is part of their culture? (In the Kanun, women are "sacks, made to endure," as if their only purpose is to bear men's children—male children, preferably.) These traditions are dying out, I imagine. But what will I make of the vestiges that remain?

And can I stick it out for a year? How hard will life in Kosovo be? Will there be enough food? Will we be able to find decent housing? Can we stay healthy? We spoke recently with a psychologist who took a team of his fellows into Kosovo last winter. Seven of the ten got viral pneumonia, several became extremely depressed, and only one is willing to return.

How dangerous will it be? Only today I read a news report about a Bulgarian U.N. worker in the capital, Prishtina, who, being stopped on the street by an Albanian who asked the time in Serbian, politely answered in the same language. Believing he had identified one of the hated Serbs, the Albanian shot the young Bulgarian to death. The U.N. worker's only mistake was giving the time in the language of the enemy. Political correctness, Balkan style.

Ed has taken unpaid leave from the law school to work *pro bono* in the Balkans and I've resigned from my marketing job of twelve years. We will have no income for a year, but we've decided to make the commitment. The only worry that really remains tonight is whether I can do anything useful for the Kosovars. I don't want to be a voyeur in a country that has suffered so much. Ed will be helping to create a modern legal system with the American Bar Association's Central and Eastern European Law Initiative (ABA-CEELI). But I have no legal training, no medical or counseling skills. And there is certainly no need in Kosovo at this stage for my marketing experience.

But I did spend the last four weeks, day and night, working to get a certificate in teaching English as a second language. Will I be able to do that? Would that be useful? It is all unknown. As Daddy would say, I'm "borrowing trouble." I'll just have to see what happens.

Friday, August 25, 2000

Tomorrow we leave for D.C. for a few days, then Kosovo. And tonight I feel so sad to be leaving our sweet little house on the cliff over the ocean, my friends and family, our cat, Rodney. We've put our personal stuff in the studio, preparing the house for our tenant. I find myself envying her the next year in our house, the beautiful views, the ocean air.

I've solved my biggest worry by buying Web TV for my parents. With no phone system and no mail in Kosovo, the only way to communicate with them will be through satellite internet. They are old and Daddy's lung cancer, though in remission, could come back at any time. Now that they have access to the web, I know they can reach me if they have to. And they have actually become enthusiastic about the trip.

In our living room sit ten bulging suitcases, our life for the next year. I've packed so many means of diversion: books, CDs, pencils and paints, my harmonica (piano substitute) . . . Many of the books are about Kosovo, the history of the Balkans area, texts to help us understand better where we are going and what's happening there. But I'm also taking with me Lord Peter Wimsey, Jeeves, Sherlock Holmes, and I wonder, am I bringing with me the bricks and mortar of my own fortifications, the walls to keep fear away, to isolate myself from the place, the people, the chaos? Should I leave it all behind? Should I fearlessly embrace the conditions I've been told to expect, the long silent nights, the turmoil on the streets, the gunfire, with only the contents of my brain (and my character, God help me) to get me through? Should I forego the idea of diversion altogether and throw myself naked into the experience?

Writer Gretel Ehrlich of her sojourn in Greenland: "I close my eyes for the moment but the brightness penetrates my eyelids. Light peels my skin; the hole in the ozone stares at me. There is nothing more to lose or gain. Empty-handed I climb out of my own hole to some other kind of observation post. Exposure implies vision. Isn't that the point of travel? To stumble, drop one's white cane in a blizzard and learn to see."

Yes, well, Gretel, I know you're right. And I wish I could put it so eloquently. But I'm hanging on to my cane for a while yet. Lord Peter may come in handy on those dark, Balkan nights.

FRIDAY, SEPTEMBER 1, 2000
Prishtina, Kosovo

We arrived this afternoon around 3. From Ljubljana, Slovenia, the pilot headed west and south, over the Adriatic almost to Brindisi, Italy, then back east to Kosovo. All to avoid Serbian air space. I walk through the curtains of business class into coach, headed for the john, and, with a shock, discover a sea of young, dark-haired men, all staring at me, neither friendly nor unfriendly, just intent . . . on something. Are they returning refugees? During the fighting and ethnic cleansing of 1998 and 1999, the Kosovo diaspora took refugees to all parts of the globe—now many are being forced out of their host countries, returning to whatever uncertain future their devastated country offers. Or are they simply business travelers in casual clothes?

In our business-class cabin, everyone is Western European or American—some with guns and extra clips at the waist, a good indication that the usual rules won't apply here. And all men, again, save me.

Below us lie rugged mountains whose slopes and valleys are dotted with isolated villages. Their bright red roofs, so the man next to us says, signal the massive reconstruction going on here. Almost half of the Albanian homes in Kosovo were destroyed by the Serbs, he tells us, not as a result of the "collateral damage" of war, but as a result of the calculated plan to drive Kosovo Albanians from their homes and from the country, to create a country for Serbs. All over the country, he says, homes are being rebuilt with international aid.

As we descend toward Prishtina we see in the devastated Serb military complexes the effectiveness of the three-month-long NATO bombing campaign of the spring of 1999, and on the outskirts of the city we see hundreds of houses burned and gutted by Serb and Yugoslav forces. And then we begin to see camouflage on tanks, helicopter gunships, bunkers, gun emplacements, armored personnel carriers, men. The reassuring camouflage of KFOR (Kosovo-Force, the United Nations–authorized, NATO–led military force in Kosovo). As we taxi up to the terminal, I see a tiny hand-lettered sign over the terminal door that reads "Welcome to Prishtina."

We are entering the first country to be completely administered by the United Nations. Since June 1999, when NATO forces drove out the ruling Serbs, the U.N. and KFOR have been running Kosovo and protecting it from any further Serb incursions. They have responsibility for everything from roads to the judicial system to schools to the police, and will have until the "final disposition" of Kosovo can be determined.

I am the first person off the plane, walking down the steps onto the tarmac as if it was all familiar ground. This strange familiarity comes, no doubt, from our culture's frequent exposure to war and its trappings in movies and on TV. The real and unreal have become so blurred in even my mind—I who see relatively little of this stuff—that what should shock seems only a memory of something experienced in a safe and cozy room. Is that why I feel no fear, or is it because my curiosity is so strong it drives out fear? Soldiers, policemen everywhere. Men with guns. I look back to see some poohbah from our cabin being greeted on the tarmac by effusions of handshakes and photographs. We discover later it is probably his presence that has caused KFOR to block the locals' presence from the terminal, their cars from the airport. And outside the terminal another crowd of young males. Now and again there is an older face, thin, sunken cheeks and flowing mustache, all topped by the *plis,* the country's traditional white felt conical cap worn by Kosovo's patriarchs. But no women at all. What are all these guys doing here? Not waiting for relatives' arrivals as far as I can tell. Just passing the time, checking to see who's come into their country?

Ed makes ten laborious trips to the luggage carousel as I wait, pondering the unlikelihood of all our bags having made it to the Prishtina airport. I watch the other passengers, young Albanian men, struggle with cheap duffels that have ripped open, spilling their sartorial guts, or large cardboard boxes, once precisely rectangular and bound by twine, now smushed and shapeless, with gaping holes spewing stereo parts, blankets, stuffed toys. There is chaos here, but there seems to be a high level of tolerance for chaos. That will probably be the key to survival.

The UNMIK (United Nations Interim Administration Mission in Kosovo) customs guy, a Russian soldier, stops someone now and again, opening boxes or cases. But Ed and I don't fit his profile, and besides, he clearly has no intention of rummaging through ten large suitcases. Henry, a genial attorney from Texas who has come from the ABA-CEELI office to pick us up, assures him that Ed is here to work on the legal system. With a dismissive flip of his wrist and a question in his eyes for me ("But what are *you* doing here?"), he waves us into our new Kosovo home.

SATURDAY, SEPTEMBER 2, 2000

I feel filthy. The air is visible, dust and soot—an unfiltered coal power plant outside of town belches huge black clouds into the air—the acrid smell of garbage burning, the stench of rotting food littering streets and sidewalks. Inside, the Grand Hotel smells the same but with the addition of cigarette smoke. My throat is raw already, my hair matted. With Ed's driver, Hajriz, we go out looking at houses for rent on Dragodan Hill, the Pacific Heights of Prishtina. Ed's office is here. From a distance the hill looks good—large buildings, red tile roofs. Up close, Dragodan is a mess. Few houses look finished—all are either being torn down or having rooms and stories built on. Glassless windows stare at the neighbors. Construction materials spill over into the streets, the ubiquitous hollow red building blocks fragile, already crumbling before they are put up. My brother David would enjoy seeing the construction methods here. Patios and floors under construction are supported by a small forest of saplings, cut and stuck under the slab just as God created them, bark, knobs, warps and all, a couple of feet apart. Nothing looks quite plumb. This city would surely be flattened in an explosion of dust by an earthquake.

We walk through several houses, but decide to look again tomorrow.

We are staying in the Grand Hotel, a Tito-era monstrosity. We looked at three rooms before finding, like Goldilocks, the one that is "just right." Or as close to just right as one could get in the Grand. Room not too hot, bed not too saggy, carpets not as filthy as others, though it doesn't pay to look too closely. In the bathroom, the plastic trash basket has been used by some poor former resident with diarrhea. I kick it out the door and into the charwomen's area. Vacuuming is not part of the daily cleaning, we've been told, though changing the sheets is. We can look forward to clean white sheets each day, and, though they're the texture of fine sandpaper, they are spotless.

A sign in the lobby of the Grand says "Dear Guests. Grand Hotel is reconstructing. Apologize for disturbance!" But I've read a couple of books written before the war that describe the Grand Hotel, and I would say the only things that have been "reconstructed" are the new Otis elevators replacing the ones Robert Kaplan describes in *Balkan Ghosts* as looking like "grafitti-scarred toilet stalls." The thin, buckling carpets are the color of rancid pea soup and the concrete walls, both inside and out, are rapidly decomposing.

The Grand was headquarters for Arkan, the sociopathic Serb paramilitary leader who was assassinated recently in Belgrade. He used the lower floor as his "interrogation" center. We have already heard gruesome tales of torture, rape, and murder here.

Shots now and then below us. A single shot. Or five rapid shots followed quickly by five more. Celebrations? Or something else.

Always the sounds of children below, laughing, squealing, being children.

Last night, in the few minutes before I was overwhelmed by sleep, I heard cars honking over and over, people laughing, still finding pleasure in each other, the vibrancy of a city still alive. And this morning, awakened at 5 by the call to prayer from the city's mosques, and later by the sounds of children playing, of traffic stirring. This city of 200,000 before the war, now at 400,000, the excess mostly refugees and international workers, groping its way toward Normal.

And tonight through our open window . . . John Fogerty? Yes. Creedence Clearwater: "Bad Moon Rising" from someplace across the noisy main thoroughfare. It's Saturday night and sounding like a weekend in any city. Ed crashed about 5 from jet lag. I go downstairs at 8 to the hotel dining room where I find a handful of diners—all internationals—in a vast cavernous room with maybe a hundred tables covered by crisp linen tablecloths. The lamb chops are fatty but taste like lamb—more than I can say for Safeway lamb at home. Peas soft and mushy. The single brussels sprout very tasty. The waiter kindly helps me with the pronunciation of "hello," "*Toongyetyeta*" phonetically.

Now, Bob Dylan's "knock, knock, knockin' on heaven's door" blasting up from below as I write.

Now, "Twist and Shout."

A street party for international soldiers and policemen.

I walk through the sepulchral hotel halls reeking of cigarette smoke and out onto the street to the net café but don't feel uneasy. Even at night on these womenless streets. Maybe I should. Certainly I won't go far from the Grand by myself, not yet. Not until I learn what's safe and what's not.

The friendly net café manager, Osman, helps me with "Thank you." He writes "*Me nder qofshi.*" I blanche. The book says it's "*Ju falemnderit.*" Either way, too many consonants!

I've had a couple of moments of doubt in the last two days—*What are we doing here?* As I glance back at our sweet home on the ocean, the ridge, the bay, San Francisco sparkling in the distance, I think: A year of my life. Here. In the smoke and dust and stench, surrounded by men with guns.

But, examining myself tonight, I am astonished to find that the fears I suffered in the months before we left home have disappeared. Replaced, maybe, by curiosity or excitement, or maybe by the simple necessity of my "To Do" list. Whatever the reason, from the moment I set foot on the airport tarmac, I have felt no fear—only eager anticipation.

MONDAY, SEPTEMBER 4, 2000

Blackbirds are everywhere in Prishtina. At 5 this morning I'm awakened by the call to prayer, haunting in its five-note range, the call coming through a din of blackbird cries, must be thousands of them, the clear tones of the singer and the birds' cries so intertwined that I hear the voice echoing among the birds long after the song has ended. Not far from here, in 1389 on what the Serbs call *Kosovo Polje,* the Field of the Blackbirds, the trouble started, at least according to Serbian mythology. On that field Serb-led forces suffered a defeat by the Ottoman Turks, a defeat made glorious in legend and epic poem and used by Serb ideologues of the last century to create a holy ground in Kosovo. The Serbs' Jerusalem. On the six hundredth anniversary of the battle, in 1989, Slobodan Milosevic spoke to hundreds of thousands of impassioned Serbs gathered on the Field of the Blackbirds. Here he combined his hateful nationalist rhetoric with the mythical symbolism of that field to identify ethnic Albanians with the hated Turks, to brand Kosovo onto the hearts of the Serbs, to reassert eternal domination. That moment was the beginning of a brutal ten-year repression in Kosovo that led to last year's tragedy, and to our presence here, Ed's and mine, today.

I doze and at 7:30 a.m. awakened again by some Middle Eastern pop music followed quickly by the deep *thump-thump* of American rap. I long for an encore by the Muslim muezzin.

WEDNESDAY, SEPTEMBER 6, 2000

We have been in our new Prishtina house two days now. The décor of the house, so shocking to me when we first saw it, is already unremarkable. The anarchy of the streets outside is also beginning to seem normal.

We looked for a house a second day, still not knowing what we should expect. A good bed, a big refrigerator, central heat, a dishwasher, a bathtub? Should we expect it to be clean, roofed, furnished, secure? Most places were too-something: big, small, filthy, inconvenient, expensive. One had been rented to some young men from Oxfam who, in the universal fashion of young men, had left quite a mess.

The last house we saw seemed to be a remnant of the Ottoman

Empire at its most decadent: tufted red velvet sofas sweeping around two walls of the upstairs parlor, a bright red Persian-style carpet, white long-haired wooly throws flung around on sofas and floors, peacock feathers in purple vases, huge heavy chandeliers that Ed immediately characterized as Neo-Ottoman-Baroque. An ornate Russian samovar adorned a side table. The bedroom boasted heavily lacquered furniture and the face of a ferociously growling tiger on the velour bedspread. True, the house was spotless, was the right size, and the owners seemed friendly, but . . . We turned to our translator and asked, "Is this décor normal? Is this a *good* rental?"

"Oh, yes!" Loriana replied. "This is one of the nicest I've seen. You should take it right away before anyone else gets it."

So at the end of the day, with much trepidation, I fetch Ed, an interpreter, and the driver and go back to say we'll take it. Isa and his wife, Igballe, are our landlords. Isa says the rent is 3,000 Deutschemarks a month. About $1,500. (The competition among the thousands of internationals for good space in safe areas is keen, and has driven prices up to appalling figures.) We pay for utilities, and Igballe will mop and vacuum for us once a week. They will live in an apartment in the house but won't bother us, he assures us. We will keep the front entrance for ourselves, and will have the two main floors of the house. He wants 1,000 DM to hold it until we get our contract and first month's rent to him, but when it's clear we don't have that much on hand—we haven't had our dollars changed yet—he quickly comes down to 200 DM and with a handshake we have a deal.

The next day Ed and I go to the ABA-CEELI office where we piece together a contract, get it translated into Albanian by Ed's bright young translator, Blerta, then send Hajriz out to change dollars to Deutschemarks. By 5:30, Blerta, Hajriz, Isa and Igballe, Ed and I are sitting at their dining table for the signatures, the ceremonial eating of candied apricots Igballe proudly serves us, and the smiles all round. Isa tells us he knows his house isn't as nice as what we're used to. I assure him we think they have a beautiful home and that we're very happy to have found it. He says he thinks we'll be very happy here. We think so too.

Despite our doubts about the house, it has been an easy, amiable transaction.

Blerta asks if it's normal for both Ed and me to sign contracts. In Kosovo, women have few property rights—or much of anything else—and so it seems strange that the lease speaks of tenants in the plural, and both of us are signing, when only Isa is signing as owner. Ed assures Blerta that in the U.S. men and women share property rights—and responsibilities—and that this is normal. Blerta nods appreciatively. "Is very good," she says.

We go back to Ed's office, grab our many bags with the help of our friends, and by 6:30 are moved in. I am thrilled—though I do admit embarrassment at having so much luggage. "The ugly American strikes again," I murmur, looking with dismay at our bags, but Hajriz, having heard and understood, says with a smile, "No, is O.K."

Isa and Igballe have no English. Ed and I have no Albanian. We get along through a few shared words of French with Isa, a lot of sign language and mime, and an abundance of goodwill.

Isa must have been a popular, mischievous boy. He still flashes an infectious smile. He is shorter than Igballe, and stocky, with white hair and darkish skin. Although our interpreter tells us he's a banker, he looks like a farmer, or a loyal Communist functionary (indeed, we find the complete works of Marx and Lenin in the bookshelf). Igballe looks more sophisticated, and is, in fact, a teacher. A pleasant, attractive woman with short black hair standing up stiffly from her forehead. They seem to regard each other with affection.

I do wonder, though, how they feel about moving out of their home. It must be hard for them, for Igballe in particular, who, as she shows us her freshly ironed linens, the full set of Bulgarian dishes, the new blue and white tiles in the bathroom, seems very "house-proud." But they don't seem resentful. I think they are so happy with the money, and that they have tenants they can trust with the house—so they tell us—that they feel they have the best of all worlds.

That night the four of us scramble—Ed and I to get our stuff assembled in some orderly fashion, Igballe and Isa to get their clothes out of the closets and drawers. In the midst of all this, the electricity goes off. Laughing, we all improvise. Igballe gets a battery-powered lantern and a candle. I find my flashlight. We get things done.

It is already clear that the only way to survive Kosovo daily life is to develop that tolerance for chaos the local people seem to have. If a meeting doesn't start for hours because someone's driver didn't show or the participants didn't get the word, it's normal and not a problem. If there's no water, or no electricity, or the pipe under the sink leaks after one day of use, that's normal and not a problem. If the box of salt leaks all over the floor because it's not seamed properly or the stove top takes fifteen minutes to heat up or the hose from the washing machine disconnects, flooding the bathroom floor, that's normal and not a problem. If it *is* a problem, you've got a problem.

THURSDAY, SEPTEMBER 7, 2000

Prishtina is a city of fragments. There are few whole things here— few intact surfaces, few complete buildings, few functional systems. Concrete sidewalks are split and buckled, stuccoed walls are crazed and stained, roads are gullied and pocked with holes big enough to swallow a small car, steps are crumbling, ragged-edged. Turgid, smelly gray-water seeps from every crack and pit. And everywhere, everywhere, garbage. Piles of it along every block, spilling out of cans and Dumpsters, rotting, stinking, a feeding-ground for feral dogs and cats. Twentieth-century Prishtina is like a medieval town where the only objective was to get the garbage out of the house—nobody cared what happened to it after that.

I know from my own experience that we travelers can sometimes make the mistake of looking at poverty and calling it "quaint." Maybe because a beauty of color or line or texture, or the rich patina that sometimes comes with the great age of a building or town, can hide the misery of its inhabitants. Prishtina, permanently defaced by grim Communist-era concrete office and apartment blocks, is not one of those places. No one could make the mistake of calling Prishtina "quaint."

Last year's Serb–NATO war itself is not the culprit. Except for looting and vandalism—and the forced expulsion of the Albanian residents, of course—the Serbs left Prishtina largely alone (they needed it, after all), and NATO conducted only a few "surgical" strikes in the city to destroy Serbian police and military capability. The cause of the bedlam is much more complex: Tito-era apartment and office buildings that started to deteriorate before they were finished; a cultural tradition of adding bits and pieces onto one's house as extra money becomes available so that most houses have rooms, stories, that are only partially finished, and may stay that way for months or years or forever; the local habit of tossing trash onto the streets; the failure of UNMIK and OSCE (Organization for Security and Cooperation in Europe) to effectively organize for such basic amenities as street repair and garbage pickup. A neighbor, a charming young man named Sulejman, tells me Prishtina is not as "nice" as it once was because "the people from the country-side have come and they have no manners. They write graffiti on the walls and make a big mess." One of our drivers, a handsome young man named Fexhi, agrees with this diagnosis. The refugees from the countryside, he says, have ruined the city. But Jehona, Ed's legal assistant, a strikingly beautiful young law student of twenty-three, dismisses this theory as simply a new urban myth, the result of the city-dweller's prejudice against the peasant. "We have always had garbage," she says. "It is one of the worst parts of our country. I hope you won't judge us too harshly because of all this trash."

But certainly much of the confusion, and much of the daily de-bris, comes from the simple fact of a city built to hold 200,000 sud-denly bursting with 400,000. Too many cars, too many people, too much refuse, too much confusion. It's amazing anything works at all.

This afternoon we walk along Prishtina's "Champs Elysées," Mother Teresa Boulevard. (Mother Teresa was born in Kosovo, though she grew up in Macedonia.) Small shops and restaurants line the street on either side. A fountain sits in a mini-park, in its center a concrete statue of a stylized woman, hands outstretched, in better days offering a stream of water to boulevardiers. Now her hands hold a banana peel and a Coke can, and her skirts are edged with plastic bags and crumpled cigarette packages. In the best tra-dition of European cities, there are trees lining the street. Planted, no doubt, to lend an air of elegance to the boulevard, they seem now to struggle simply to survive. But maybe that's all that's needed now. It is enough to survive.

Scores of kiosks and tables dot the sidewalks offering a motley assortment of cigarettes, CDs (or CD rip-offs—the best copies of any American pop artist for about two dollars each), combs, Snick-ers bars, cigarette lighters, socks, books and pamphlets on Albanian history, posters of KLA (Kosovo Liberation Army) heroes and

martyrs. The sidewalks are crowded, mostly young men just hanging out. With 75 percent unemployment, and houses and apart-
ments full to overflowing because of the refugee crisis, there is little
for these young men to do here but hang out on the streets and
watch the colorfully Spandexed teenaged girls strut their stuff. It is
clear these young women feel no restraints from an Islamic dress
code. But many older women, always walking in twos, wear traditional long shapeless coat-dresses and cover their hair with scarves.
All these strollers carry their shopping in the thin plastic bags that,
within an hour, will be littering streets all over Prishtina.

We came here expecting a scarcity of "stuff"—clothes, toiletries,
household necessities. That was the case a few months ago. Now,
though, enterprising merchants have opened or reopened scores of
shops offering many of the things we need. And more shops open,
literally, daily. It looks to me as if it is the international community
that is driving this new capitalism, for we are the ones with money
and there are thousands—maybe tens of thousands?—of us here,
and we have brought our consumer habits with us. Pizzerias and
cappuccino bars cater to our culinary cravings. A small bookstore
on Mother Teresa offers a modest assortment of literary classics
and a few magazines in English, French, and German, as well as Albanian. And, as in the U.S., almost every block has its shoe store full
of Adidas and Nike, or at least shoes with Adidas and Nike labels.

I have discovered a market, Ardi, that caters to internationals.
Butter, cheese, breakfast cereal (though only one that is not "cocoa-
flavored"), soups, seasonings, candy and cookies, soft drinks, sham-
poo, fruit yogurt, canned mushrooms and olives, and pasta, lots of
pasta. I can hardly believe my luck today—they have skinless, bone-
less chicken breasts in the new freezer. Processed in China, approved for use by Muslims, according to the English-language label.

I stoop to examine some bags of what I hope is flour. (The label is in the Cyrillic alphabet so I can decipher nothing. It *feels* like flour.) I feel something nudging my arm and look over to see the barrel of an assault rifle pointed at the floor beside me. And a pair of heavy black boots topped by camouflage pants. "Ah, excuse me, Madam!" says the young soldier, a Brit. He is off duty for a moment, I guess, and still carries his automatic weapon even while buying salt (for that is what he chooses from the shelf).

A reminder that I'm not at Safeway anymore.

Later . . .
Ed is hosting a seminar for defense attorneys in Prishtina, and tonight we are entertaining one of the speakers, a bright, amiable judge who has flown in from the Netherlands to provide a Western European legal perspective. The restaurant we take him to specializes in beef smothered in various sauces, and is the best we've seen. As we chat, Margaret, an American who works with OSCE, drops by our table. "Paula," she says, "several of us 'internationals' have decided that your presence in Kosovo indicates things are getting back to normal." Ed and I have become celebrities of sorts, she says, he for bringing a spouse, the first, and me for coming with him. The state department, OSCE, the U.N., and other organizations don't permit "spouses" on the Kosovo assignment, for it has been designated both a "hardship" and a "dangerous" post. But I think all this will begin to change soon. More consumer goods are arriving daily, more roads are being repaired, and food, though limited in scope, is plentiful. So it doesn't feel like "hardship" to me. Maybe "inconvenience post" is more accurate. This place simply requires us to constantly adjust, adapt, and improvise. (Of course, we haven't hit winter yet. I expect I'll be crying "hardship" when the temperature is 20 below and there's no heat.)

Ed and I are here, after all, more than a year after the war ended, months after the worst of the refugee crisis. Most people are fed now, and many of the houses and villages are being rebuilt. There is enough warm clothing for the winter in most places. The sandals and blue-jeans crowd, those brave, resourceful emergency aid workers, are beginning to leave, and the suits are showing up, those of us who are here to help the Kosovars keep the peace and build a country.

And is it still a "dangerous post"? Well, yes, though not as much for internationals as for locals. The upcoming municipal elections have spawned assassinations of candidates in towns outside of Prishtina. The U.S. Mission issues warnings of all sorts: *Don't* wander off the main roads, *Don't* walk alone if you have to go out at night, *Don't* travel to certain parts of the country. Ed has posted in his office their most recent memo warning that there were four shootings and six "controlled detonations of suspected explosive devices" last week. Pistols, hand grenades, and automatic weapons are common, and the potential for ethnic violence is still high. And as in any postwar area, there are lots of crazies hanging around. We will maintain a high level of vigilance—but, hopefully, will keep it short of paranoia.

Outside UNMIK headquarters downtown is a terrifying display of land mines and other explosive devices, with warnings that thousands of them—unexploded—still lie in wait for the unwary throughout the country. Posters warning parents and children of these devices are plastered all over town, and indeed, several of the devices on display look like toys. One, the "Blu 397," is a small, bright-yellow canister with fan blades on top. If I were a seven-year-old child, I would want to twirl those blades, toss the can into the sky, and see it float down like a helicopter. There have been, the sign says, 2,937 of these found so far. Many, no doubt, were discovered when they were stepped on by civilians, perhaps children. . . .

FRIDAY, SEPTEMBER 8, 2000

Today we go with Henry to Skopje, Macedonia, the safe haven for internationals, the place where one banks, buys office supplies, groceries, clothes, Big Macs. Our driver, Fexhi, who is as sweet and shy as he is handsome, manipulates the car around potholes, 16-wheelers, and armed personnel carriers as if the car were simply another appendage of his body. After forty-five minutes or so, the flat country begins to rise into a range of hills, then mountains. Beautiful country.

Frequently we see armed camps, KFOR bases surrounded by walls of sandbags and barbed wire. A convoy passes us—buses and cars full of men, women, and children accompanied by armed personnel carriers and truckloads of troops. Fexhi tells us these are Serbs, being escorted through Albanian territory by their international guards. Well over two thirds of the Serb inhabitants of Kosovo, some 200,000, fled the country after NATO drove the Yugoslav and Serbian forces out in June 1999. Those who remain live mostly in Serb-only enclaves, rarely venturing outside their homes, and never traveling without the protection of KFOR. Each Serbian Orthodox church we pass—ancient, graceful, domed, and arched—is sandbagged, surrounded by barbed wire, and guarded by at least one tank. An unguarded church is likely to be destroyed by vengeful Albanians who see the Serbian Orthodox Church as a principal instigator of Serbian ambitions in Kosovo. I've heard estimates that some eighty churches have been blown up since the end of the war.

We reach the border where, Henry says, we must get out of our Kosovo-registered car, cross no-man's-land on foot, and hire a taxi at the Macedonian side. I ask Henry why we can't just continue in our own car. "Macedonia has just made it illegal for cars registered in Kosovo to cross into their territory," he tells us. "The Macedonian Slav majority don't like Albanians much—and don't want any more of them in the country. About a third of the population is Albanian, and that's too much already for the Macedonian government!" We find a cab, but Henry is clearly disgusted with it—the filthy sheepskin covering the back seat, the scores of flies buzzing around our heads. There has been a sheep in the car recently—we can smell it. Henry complains to the driver, who simply shrugs and slips the car into gear.

We get into Skopje and pull up to the bank, which is strangely dark and lifeless. Our driver shrugs again, this time with a sly smile at Henry's increasing bad humor. It's Macedonia's Independence Day, it seems. The bank and all stores are closed. We have spent a whole day and have gotten nothing useful done. But I wouldn't have missed this trip for the world.

SATURDAY, SEPTEMBER 9, 2000

When I come downstairs for coffee this morning, Ed announces that Igballe had come by wanting to clean the house, but he convinced her to come back on Monday since I was still asleep. Impressed, I ask how he was able to communicate all that. Oh, we went through all the days of the week and settled on that one, he says. Good, I'll sleep in a bit longer. At 11 precisely, after Ed is gone, Igballe knocks on the door, bucket and mop in hand, ready to clean. So much for the days of the week in Albanian. And typical of our attempts at communication.

Our first "diplomatic" party tonight. We walk the steps down Dragodan Hill to the Grand Hotel where we meet friends in the lobby, then walk the few blocks to the nightclub where a going-away party is being held for a top OSCE official. Speeches are already underway when we arrive. Long, flowery speeches, the tradition here, made even longer by translation, a phrase at a time, into Albanian, French, Serbian, English, Russian—at least two translations going for each speaker. The honoree speaks movingly of last year's horrors here in Prishtina, when the Serb military and paramilitaries began murdering civilians and forcing tens of thousands of Albanian residents out of their homes and out of the country. When the NATO bombs started to drop. When the OSCE monitoring offices were finally evacuated. The large cocktail party crowd becomes silent as he reminisces about that terrible time, a time many of these here also remember.

After the speeches, Ed is introduced to an American working for OSCE who corners him into a dinner meeting on Monday night to discuss Rule of Law projects they might do together. Among other things, they will be trying to teach judges and defense attorneys whose only education and experience was with a Communist legal system, and who, in any case, were not allowed to practice at all during the last ten years. Now, Ed will join the effort to bring these Kosovar judges and lawyers up to speed on the European Convention on Human Rights, as well as other human rights conventions. The task is unbelievably daunting, and I know Ed is preparing for twelve- to fifteen-hour workdays.

The international prosecutor from the still-violent city of Mitrovica arrives—a larger-than-life, burly, bearded American lawyer surrounded by several armed bodyguards, grim men with psychopathic eyes. The prosecutor is trying Serbs accused of war crimes in a northern city full of Serbs, so the bodyguards are not mere window-dressing. Death threats are a regular part of his life; last week eleven Serbs indicted for war crimes escaped from the jail in Mitrovica and disappeared. The prosecutor tells Ed he wants to go back to the U.S. to teach law and Ed tells him he would never be happy in a law school after . . . this. How could he ever get his adrenaline level raised this high again?

Monday, September 11, 2000

Prishtina is a bowl with scalloped edges. At the bottom of the bowl lies the downtown with its sprawl of dilapidated apartment blocks built with the Communist determination to sacrifice form to function. A testimony to an era of corrupt or incompetent contractors and city officials, these buildings are falling apart (it can't be too soon). But rising all around the flat center are hills, and here the city softens. I look from the steps of Dragodan over to the other hills beyond downtown, and with their red tile roofs in the late afternoon sun, they seem to glow. Everything is better seen at a distance here.

Our street address means nothing because there are no street signs, and the names changed from Albanian to Serbian in 1989 and, theoretically, back to Albanian last year. So no one is quite sure what is where. Although Dragodan is a "nice" area, it is essentially a shambles. We are one street down from the top of the hill, high enough to escape most of the dust and pollution downtown, but the air is still hard to breathe. The street itself is made of cut stone and the houses along it are large—several bedrooms each—most in a state of disrepair or construction. The houses across the street and next door to us, like a hundred other houses on Dragodan, are being expanded and remodeled to attract internationals, so piles of hollow red bricks and lumber clutter most of the tiny yards. Yet there are flowers growing around the piles of bricks and debris— beautiful, fragrant roses in almost every yard, insisting on their right to flourish even amid the clutter.

Between our house and Ed's office, a ten-minute walk further up the hill, are three tiny grocery stores. Built into garage space in front of the houses, these stores offer essentials to the immediate neighborhood: milk, cookies and candy bars, eggs, potatoes and onions, and, for internationals, bottled water. Across the street from our house is the store belonging to Orhan, a red-faced, white-haired gentleman who insists on trying to communicate with me in German, though I've tried to explain I'm as helpless in that language as in Albanian. He would like to be grumpy, but is a reluctant sweetheart. His wife has kindly taken me into their house to explain (in French) what products I need to use in our dishwasher. Up the street is another slightly larger store, this one run by a sweet-faced young woman named Lulja, who shyly practices her English with me and insists on exchanging the red peppers I've chosen for other, better ones. And close to Ed's office is Fatmir's store, where he and Abdullah, his assistant, proudly display what they say is the best variety of chocolate candies in the area. As I walk between home and office each day I wave to these new friends and they, sitting always at their counters and rarely distracted by customers, smile and wave back.

Today Ed and I walk Qeni, the office dog (abandoned and starving when one of the staff rescued him), along the dirt road at the crest of Dragodan. There's a soccer field here where young boys play, and next to the field lies a small copse, a wood of slender trees just beginning to look like fall. A peaceful place, the first such we've seen here. But somewhere on this hill over a hundred Kosovo Albanian civilians, victims of a massacre, were buried by retreating Serbs in a mass grave that was discovered just a few months ago. Ed's office has taken part in the investigation and in the identification of bodies. So even this quiet hilltop harbors a horrible history. It is hard to escape the burden of history in this country; we are ambushed by it each time we turn a corner, climb a hill.

Government agencies and NGOs (non-governmental organizations) from all over the world have sprung up like weeds all over Dragodan. Houses around us have been converted to headquarters for Oxfam, International Organization for Migration, Council of Europe, the Danish Mission, the British Mission, World Vision,

United Nations Committee for Refugees, Churches Acting Together, DAC (an explosives ordnance disposal outfit), and many,
many others. Their vans and SUVs are everywhere; sometimes it
seems that the entire world is here in this small city in Kosovo. I
have heard, in fact, that there are five hundred non-governmental
organizations in the country. It's beginning to feel strange and uncomfortable. Unwelcome skepticism arises—in both Ed and me.
What are all these internationals doing? Are we all just talking to
each other? Passing paperwork from one NGO to the next, coming
up with projects that fulfill grant requirements but have no real ef-
fect on the Kosovars? Are we driving our big SUVs from one office
to another, never stopping to talk with the people who live here?
We'll find out what's going on. But for now, the sheer number of
international organizations and our dominance of the local landscape make me uneasy. Very uneasy.

TUESDAY, SEPTEMBER 12, 2000

10 p.m. Ed's at dinner with the attorneys he's been teaching. I'm
at home in bed. The electricity went out an hour ago, so my tiny
battery-powered book light is the only illumination in the house. A
generator growls and clanks next door. A few minutes ago I heard
gunshots. Somewhere down the street people are singing. It is beginning to rain. I am living in a fascinating country. I have never felt
so alive.

THURSDAY, SEPTEMBER 14, 2000

I am so nervous! Tomorrow I interview for a teaching position at
the Cambridge School (no relation to the university), one of the

privately owned English-language schools in town. I've been reviewing tenses, practicing answers to potential questions. I don't know a thing about the school and have no idea if this is what I should do in Kosovo. Or if, after tomorrow's interview, I'll even get the chance to do it. Will they hire an American whose only teaching experience was in history thirty years ago?

Meanwhile, I help Ed set up his office. I'm doing the financial reports as Ed tries to get some things working. And *nothing* is working. The phone landlines don't work. The mobile phones don't have chips, and Alcatel chips, the only kind that work in this country, are carefully rationed by the telephone company. Ed's been told there are no more available. The satellite internet is not working either, so other agencies' communications with ABA-CEELI have to be done through courier. The generator is on the blink, the Jeeps are not registered or licensed or insured and so, technically, mustn't be driven. Because it's an all-cash economy—no bank, no credit cards, no checks—Ed has to drive to the bank in Macedonia to bring in $10,000 at a time to operate the office. He locks it up in the filing cabinet and disperses it as needed. (Lately some of the larger NGOs have been burglarized, their safes dropped from second- and third-story windows to accomplices below.) Ed has spent most of his time so far trying to put together functioning systems so he can get to the real work he came to do.

Right now, Ed's the only American at the ABA-CEELI office. The two who were here last year have left, and the other attorneys who will work with him won't arrive until October. But he gets lots of help and moral support from the local staff, warm, generous young men and women who try to make us feel at home.

As I work with Ed this afternoon, I think about what it was that brought him here. I remember his shock as Bosnia and Croatia were ravaged by Serbian forces in the early '90s, and later when they started raping, killing, and driving hundreds of thousands of Kosovo Albanians from their homes in 1998. "I can't believe that at the end of the twentieth century we're allowing genocide to happen in Europe again!" he said, over and over during that time. He was relieved when the U.S. and Britain finally led NATO in driving the Serbs out of Kosovo in the spring of 1999. But it was not enough for Ed. I remember clearly the day, a year later, when he said to me, "Surely there's something we can do. . . ." And the "we" he used was not a universal "we." He meant Ed and Paula.

So here we are today trying to cobble together a functioning office for his work in Kosovo. I don't think Ed really believes he can do anything of great significance here. He is a man of few illusions. But he is also a man of character and compassion. He can't just do nothing.

FRIDAY, SEPTEMBER 15, 2000

I walk into one of the classrooms with Ahmet, the owner of the Cambridge School. A tall, handsome, elegant man, he tells me after barely glancing at my résumé that he wants me to teach here. No beating around the bush. "You are an American," he says. "You are the people who helped us. You saved our lives. So you can teach our students more than English. You can teach them how to live together, with others, in peace. You can teach them how to work, how to build a democracy, how to keep trying no matter what the odds. You in America know how to do these things, and you can teach us."

Ahmet himself knows something about perseverance in the face of great loss. Both his house in the country and his apartment in Prishtina were destroyed by the Serbs, and with them, his beloved library of some five thousand books. "I'm afraid to buy books again," he says. "But I will. And the students, they must learn to love books, too, and the knowledge in books. You can teach them."

So I start a new intermediate-level class in ten days. The pay is about sixteen dollars a week, which will pay for my cab fare home each night. I hadn't intended to take a salary, but it is clear that Ahmet is pleased to be able to offer me some compensation. So I accept. Will this be the most useful contribution I can make? Can I do it well? All I know tonight is that this opportunity has been given to me, and it feels right.

SATURDAY, SEPTEMBER 16, 2000

Agim, our landlords' son, comes with his mother today to interpret for us. While Igballe vacuums, Agim and I sit in the front parlor and chat. He's a charming young man of twenty with his father's elfin eyes, and has just returned from London. After they were ordered to leave their home and their country, he and his parents went to London where their other sons live. After his parents returned to Prishtina, Agim stayed on in England for a few months. I ask why he came back. "My parents are old," he says. "Someone must be here to take care of them, to see they are O.K."

His father, he says, worked at a bank here. "He had a very important job. He went to see the factories and businesses for the bank. Not the small factories you understand, just the very biggest." Agim is proud of his father. "But then my father got back after the war and the bank is gone and he has no job anymore. So now he gets up every day, puts on his suit and walks downtown to ask the bank people if there is any work and they say no and he comes back home. He says to us, 'For thirty-five years I worked at that bank, and now I am nobody.'" Agim shakes his head and looks distraught, much as, I expect, his father looks when he comes home from the bank.

I ask what happened to his family during the war. He settles into the couch, preparing for a long story. "In 1998, you know, the Serbs started killing us big time." (Agim is proud of his English idioms.) "They drove many thousands of us from our homes. Then, in the early months of 1999, it got very, very bad. The Serbs had a plan, you know. A plan to kill Albanians, to burn our homes and make all of us leave the country. You call it ethnic cleansing. It was because of that plan that NATO helped us." In March 1999, he continues, after NATO bombs started falling on Serbian military targets in Belgrade and here in Kosovo, the Serbs stepped up the plan. One cold night, masked Serb paramilitaries broke into Agim's home and demanded that the family leave within ten minutes. Terrified, Igballe, Isa, and Agim grabbed a few things and fled, first seeking refuge with relatives in another part of the city. Then, like most others in Prishtina, they were prodded and herded onto a crowded train that took them to the Macedonian border, where international aid workers were frantically working to improvise some kind of camp for the hundreds of thousands of refugees. Eventually, because they had relatives in England, the family journeyed there for the duration of the war. "We were lucky that way."

"When we left," Agim says, "the Serbs stole everything, you know? Our car, our TV and electronic stuff, my mother's nice things. Then they killed a cat from the neighborhood, slit its throat and flung it round and round so the blood got on all the walls. My parents found the blood, and nasty things the Serbs had written on the walls, when they got home." These walls, this room, where we sit.

Agim has a job working as a guard at OSCE downtown, but he's dissatisfied. "They won't give us guns," he complains. "The international guards outside have guns, but Albanians, no! They give us only video games. So we play, and if someone breaks in, I guess we hit them on their heads with our video games!" He laughs, but is clearly not entirely happy about the situation. He is a young man, and young men here want guns.

I turn the conversation to the upcoming elections. "Ah!" he exclaims, and laughs loudly. "Every Albanian wants to be president! We will have two million presidents or two million senators. We all want to be leaders. There will be no followers!" The elections, of course, are for local officials only. Theoretically, Milosevic is still the president of the Federal Republic of Yugoslavia, which, after the bloody wars of the '90s in Croatia and Bosnia, now consists only of Serbia and Montenegro. Kosovo is, theoretically, still a province of Serbia. And the U.N. is, theoretically, administering this province now with the intention of turning it back to Serbia and Yugoslavia when things have settled down. But everyone knows this is a giant fiction. Kosovo will never be a part of Serbia again, at least as long as Milosevic is in power. Nor will it, for generations perhaps, be able to support itself, or even feed itself. After Albania, it is the poorest spot in Europe.

What is to be done with this place, with these people?

SUNDAY, SEPTEMBER 17, 2000
Prizren, Kosovo

This morning Ed and I drive to Prizren, close to the Albanian border, for a training of local defense counsel Ed has organized. Blerta, a bright, red-headed native of Albania, accompanies us, as does a professor from the university's law faculty whom Ed has enlisted to assist with the training. A quiet, dignified scholar, the professor tells us—through Blerta's translation—that when Serb military and paramilitaries started going door to door in Prishtina, his Serb neighbors urged him to leave right away lest he and his family be killed. "We thought they just wanted to protect us," he says. "After all, they were our neighbors. Our sons played soccer together. So we left. But I had forgotten my manuscript for my new book, and so I came back. And there my neighbors were, in my house, stealing everything. I had thought they were my friends."

We're staying in the Hotel Theranda, which, we're pleased to discover, is a bit cleaner than Prishtina's Grand Hotel. Middle Eastern clarinet music is blasting up from the street below, and looking out our window I can see the minarets of five mosques, including a particularly slender one with intricate stonework directly across the street. High on a hill across the river I see a Serbian Orthodox church, a lovely, graceful building with Romanesque arches and domes that looks to be, I'd say, fourteenth century. It seems to belong on this hill overlooking the ancient town, almost as if it had grown here with the pines and the cypress. Its harmonious architectural proportions are marred, I notice, by a dark, clumsy structure just in front and, squinting hard, I see that it is a KFOR emplacement—sandbags and a guardhouse. Good. It would be tragic if this lovely building were to be destroyed. Above the church, dominating the craggy crest of the hill, are the remains of a fortress which the desk clerk told me was used by Illyrians, Romans, Serbians, and Ottoman Turks.

The most striking things from our window, though, are the three huge tanks and about a dozen KFOR soldiers guarding the small stone bridge over the river. These are German soldiers in this sector of Kosovo, known for their professional, no-nonsense approach to peacekeeping.

Prizren is the kind of city that, in another country, would be a "tourist" town. It is an ancient city, one of the oldest in the country, and placed as it is on hills along a river, it is beautiful. Narrow alleys wind through the town, and there are Ottoman Turkish mosques and a lyrical multidomed stone building that was the baths four hundred years ago. But this is no tourist town. KFOR is everywhere, its presence even stronger, or at least more noticeable, than in Prishtina. And I've been told by locals not to roam the streets much beyond the river by myself, for the Albanian mafia is big here, and one of their more lucrative crimes is the abduction of women from the streets to be sold as sexual slaves in other countries, or held for ransom. Rumor, probably. And at fifty-six, I'm a tad old to be targeted as a sexual slave, but as a Western woman I might appear to be ransomable.

So I'm careful. But I do roam, of course, and am enchanted by the place. It is mysterious, more Eastern than Western, both grubby and charming. Here in Prizren it's easy to see that this part of the world has been the fault line between East and West for two thousand years, the place where opposing cultural and political forces continually met and clashed. Eastern versus western parts of the Roman Empire; the Byzantine Empire versus the Holy Roman Empire; still later the Ottoman Turks versus Europe. In our time, Eastern bloc Communism and Western capitalism played out their tug of war here, and most recently, the region has been torn between competing ethnic-based nationalisms. I can almost feel the tensions beneath my feet.

I search for intelligible landmarks. A familiar cornice or roofline, some silhouette I recognize from my European art history courses, from my life as a Westerner. I try to pin down a date, a dynasty. But just as there are few cognates in the language, so, too, there are few visual cognates. Never have I so felt the limitations of my education in "Western Civilization." The Balkans were beyond the pale of that parochial vision. I find little I can understand, but I am mesmerized by the mystery of it all.

Tonight we are all together for dinner at the outdoor Fish Café by the river: two Brits, a Swede, a Netherlander, two Americans, an Albanian from Albania, and the rest Kosovo Albanians—together on this pleasant evening at our table beside the river. After a few glasses of wine, Mr. Hasanaj, a handsome older attorney with white, white hair and startling blue eyes (and who was on the Serbs' most-wanted list during the war), starts to tell jokes. In Albanian. Since some of us can't understand him he enlists the help of poor Jehona, one of Ed's legal assistants, who is sitting beside him, to translate. After a few more glasses the jokes start getting raunchy, and at last Jehona, blushing, says she can't translate them anymore. So he re-sorts to stories about Tito, and afterward, waving his index finger, says people mustn't joke about Tito, for many Kosovo Albanians still think he is a god. "It is dangerous," he says, "to joke about Tito or Stalin." "But you've been telling jokes about them," I point out. "No!" he protests, grinning. "*She's* been telling jokes about them!" pointing to his hapless translator.

He also tells us that there are fewer than two hundred Serbs re-maining in Prizren, all living close to a church near the main plaza, and closely guarded by KFOR. If the troops left, Mr. Hasanaj says with disturbing complacency, these Serbs would almost certainly be killed by local Albanians right here in the street where we sit. It oc-curs to me as he speaks that, if Tito were still in charge of things here, this ethnic violence couldn't happen. Under Tito only one identity was permissible: identity as a Yugoslav. It was only with his death that various nationalisms and ethnic hostilities began to resur-face, resulting eventually in the break-up of Yugoslavia.

After dinner, Blerim, a tall young Kosovo Albanian from Prish-tina who is serving as one of the translators for the training, corners me for what I can tell is an important conversation for him. "You must understand," he says. "Many Albanian lands were stolen from us. Our enemies drove hundreds of thousands of us out of our homes." "When was this?" I ask, realizing he's not talking about the recent war. "In the last century, and the first part of this one," he says, as passionately as if it had been yesterday. "And we were divided, we were made to live in different countries. It is our destiny that all Albanians be joined together again. And we don't need war," he hastens to add. "We will do this peacefully, by working very hard, and with the help of Western Europe and America. You must educate us and help us and show us how to work to get what we want."

People here are drunk on the blood of the past. But most Kosovars I've met know that the dream of a Greater Albania is a farfetched notion. Albania itself is even poorer than Kosovo, and has nothing to offer such a union. And Macedonia, Montenegro, other countries where Albanians live? Well, those countries wouldn't let go of any land without a fight.

Still, the Albanian flag, a black double-headed eagle on a red field, symbolizing the refusal of highland Albanians to submit to foreign conquest, flies everywhere here. Over mosques, outside stores and restaurants. It is one of the most ancient flags in Europe, having been used by the Albanian warrior hero Skanderbeg in his fight against the Ottoman Turks. This provocative symbol defies not only the Serbs, but also the U.N., which has tried to limit its display. To some it symbolizes a Greater Albania. But to almost everyone here it symbolizes an independent Kosovo, a Kosovo for Albanians.

MONDAY, SEPTEMBER 18, 2000

After today's training, three of the visiting teachers—Tim and James, trial lawyers from London, and Kees, a judge from Holland—Ed and I pile into the Jeep. Ed is driving, and we head up the river gorge in search of a way to get to the fortress at the top of the hill overlooking the town. As we drive, the gorge deepens and the river starts to run wilder. The ruins of a medieval monastery, now barbed-wired and sandbagged, straddles the river. We spot a truck going up a dirt road and decide to follow it. Another couple of vehicles are coming down, so we figure there are no land mines here. Ed stops each vehicle and asks—or tries to ask—is the fortress at the top of this hill? Ed tries English, Kees uses German, Tim tries French. Each driver, wanting to be helpful, to make us happy, only nods affirmatively and says, *"Po, po."* Yes. Yes.

Or is it *"Jo, jo"*? No, no? The words are so similar! And we remember vaguely that to some Albanians nodding means no, shaking the head means yes. We get confused. But keep going up. Toward the top we stop. Suddenly it seems we're in Switzerland. A charming tiny village is perched on the steep mountainside across from us. There are a couple of houses along our road and a store of sorts whose owner implores us to come in and buy something. Now the answer to our "Fort?" question is decidedly in the negative. "Kaput!" The universal negative. The road has stopped. We have not found the fort, but we've had an exciting drive and have seen something of the beautiful Sharri mountain country. We find out later that KFOR has taken over the fort now. Its strategic importance overlooking the town, the river, and the valley is as obvious to KFOR today as it was to the Ottoman Turks in the sixteenth century. And it's off-limits to the likes of us.

TUESDAY, SEPTEMBER 19, 2000
Prishtina, Kosovo

We drive back to Prishtina, Ed, Jehona, and I in our Jeep Cherokee. "Mom and Dad in the front seat, the kid in the back," Jehona says

gleefully. Ed is the perfect driver for these roads—his experience
4-wheeling in Utah serves us well as he jogs around potholes and
troop trucks and tractors pulling wagons carrying whole families.
Every now and then we see fresh graves close to the road, piled
high with cellophane-wrapped bouquets of flowers. KLA graves—
the Kosovo Liberation Army, the heroes of the resistance. And the
graves of local civilians killed by the Serbs, now honored as martyrs
to the Kosovo Albanian cause. Occasionally, bright orange plastic
tape marks areas still full of mines. You don't pull off the road here.

The destruction along our route is massive. Whole villages were
wiped out during the Serb rampage through the country. We see
burned mosques and schools, hundreds of burned houses and
shops. And hundreds of brand-new houses with bright orange tile
roofs, signs announcing "120 New Houses under Construction
Here" or "240 New Houses Built by . . . ," usually the work of agencies from Germany and other European Union nations. We begin
to grasp the scope of this massive rebuilding effort.

Jehona is a joy to be with, to look at. She is bright and curious
and full of fun, and she is exotic looking, with dark up-slanted eyes
and a face full of interesting angles. About an hour out of Prizren,
with some hesitation, I ask if she could tell us more of her family's
experience during the war. "I understand completely if you don't
want to talk about it," I assure her. But, like all others I've talked
with so far, Jehona is eager to tell her story. Like the others, most of
whom have volunteered their stories, she seems to consider it almost a duty to testify to the brutalities suffered by her people.

She, her sister, her brother, her cousin, and her mother (a former
Assembly member who in 1990 helped create the Kosovo independence document and was forced to live in exile during most of the
Milosevic years) were among the tens of thousands of Prishtina residents who were herded onto the trains—taking little with them—
and hauled off to the hellish dumping ground at Bllaca, close to the

Macedonian border. "We were in our apartment," she says, "and Serb police were below yelling up at us every day that all Albanians must leave. We especially worried about my brother and my cousin. They were teenaged boys, and were tall. My mother kept saying, 'Which will be more dangerous, to stay here and hope they won't find us? Or to try to leave the country? If we stay will they kill them? If we go will they kill them?'" A choice no mother should have to make. After a few days Jehona's mother decided to take their chances on the trains.

"When you were put onto the trains, you must have thought of the Holocaust and wondered if you were being taken off to be killed." "Yes," says Jehona, very matter-of-factly, "we didn't know until we got to Bllaca that they wouldn't kill the boys, and the rest of us, too." Because at that point Macedonia was refusing to take Albanian refugees, they were taken from Bllaca to a refugee camp in Albania. "It was chaos. They put families on buses, but would close the doors separating some family members from others. We tied our hands together so we couldn't be separated." After several weeks, they finally found refuge with relatives in Skopje, Macedonia. When they returned, they found their Prishtina apartment intact, but their family home in the country had been burned to the ground.

"A funny thing," she muses. "In our apartment I had two bright green baby turtles. For some reason I could not leave them. They were alive, too, you know, like us? I put them into a plastic medicine bag with a little water. I kept those turtles safe on the train, at Bllaca, in the Albanian camp and all the time we were in Macedonia. I brought them back alive to Prishtina."

Jehona ends her story, as nearly everyone who has told us their story has, "You mustn't think I had a bad time of it. What happened to me was nothing compared to what happened to many people." Ed heard this same disclaimer a few days ago from two Prishtina human rights attorneys who hid for months in barns and deserted houses, knowing that if they were recognized they would be dead. "But what happened to us was nothing," they said. "Don't think that we are complaining. . . ."

It was the country people, Jehona says, and the people in the small towns who suffered the most. Their homes, barns, and villages were burned to the ground, their livestock killed, and many thousands—no one will ever know how many—were murdered. Her elderly great-uncle and his mentally handicapped sister, who refused to leave their lifelong home in a small village, were killed. He was shot to death and Jehona thinks her great-aunt may have been burned alive in their house. Her cousin was later found in a mass grave.

But most people suffered far more than I did, she repeats.

Ed asks her, "If, when you are an attorney, you are asked to defend a Serb, would you do it?" She is silent a long time. "Do you mean a Serb who is charged with a war crime?" "I'm not specifying," Ed says. "I couldn't do it," she says at last. "Maybe in a year, two years, I could do it. But not now." "It is asking too much," I say. "No." Ed says. "It isn't asking too much, but it may be giving too much." Somehow we all seem to know what this means.

Jehona insists that we not lump Albanians in the same bag with Serbs, that we understand that the weight of the Serbs' crimes differentiates them from any retaliation some Albanians are engaging in now. "Yes," she says, "some Albanians killed Serbs, and would still like to get revenge somehow. The KLA maybe did some bad things when they tried to free Kosovo. But Albanians didn't do it like the Serbs did. Serbs came in with their army and their paramilitaries and killed us and raped us and drove us from our homes in great numbers, as a policy. Albanians didn't do that." Serb nationalists wake up every day, she declares, and think about Serbia, about what they can do to make Serbia stronger, about what they can do to get rid of the Albanians in Kosovo. When Milosevic gave the green light to Kosovo Serbs to persecute, to expel or kill their Albanian neighbors, they could have said no, but many didn't.

Jehona is only twenty-three years old, but she has been through enough—not only the war, but the ten years of oppression before that—to form passionate opinions, and she is worried about her country. She is afraid America will forget Kosovo, that America hasn't the will to stay here and help her people. You must stay, she says, and you must tell other Americans that they must come here. Without your help we cannot survive.

MONDAY, SEPTEMBER 25, 2000
Prishtina

I am jubilant! My first day teaching English in Kosovo. For years, ever since I ended my brief teaching career thirty years ago, I have had a recurring dream that I am in the classroom again, teaching a group of students *who want to learn.* It is my happiest dream and has, I know, signaled a deep longing to teach again. Today, standing in front of these young people sitting around the long table at the Cambridge School, I had a dizzying moment when I realized that that dream had, literally, come true—and in the most unlikely place in the world.

I am nervous, though. I haven't taught school in thirty years. And the Cambridge School folks have given me no guidelines, no syllabus, no rules. Just: Here's the book, good luck! But I am happy for the autonomy. There are nine students—seven teenaged boys and two girls—in this first class. More will join later, I've been told. The students are cautious and quiet, but I've come prepared with an "ice-breaker" exercise I learned at my ESL training school in San Francisco. I hand out slips of paper on which are written things like: "Find someone who is watching the Olympics every day on

TV," or "Find someone who can wiggle their ears," or "Find someone who knows how to bake a cake." They are puzzled as they
look at the slips of paper and hear my instructions, but then they
start to move around the room and ask one another the questions.
"Do you know how to wiggle your ears?" Before long everyone
is into it and the ice begins to break. Like me, they are eager to
laugh.

THURSDAY, SEPTEMBER 28, 2000

For the first time in our married life, I am ironing. Our agreement
is that, since Ed's job requires more time than mine, I will do more
of the household chores. In a mad moment I *volunteered* to do the
ironing. Today it takes me an hour and a half to iron three of his
shirts.

Later . . .
Tonight as I sit at my journal and re-read my first impressions of
the city, only a month ago, I think I may have been too harsh. I saw
then a city of fragments. Now, I'm beginning to see the whole.
What is the truth? What I saw then? Or what I am seeing now?
There's a world of difference.

SATURDAY, SEPTEMBER 30, 2000

I struggle against an overwhelming sense of isolation. Prishtina
feels like a hurricane-devastated island in the midst of a still-
turbulent sea, cut off from the rest of the world. There is no landline phone service so we can't call home, there's no postal system so

we can neither send nor receive letters and packages. We have e-mail, though it's not easily accessible. We must go to Ed's office or to a net café and hope the electricity is working and the satellite system hasn't broken down. There are few flights in and out of here—most travel has to be from Macedonia—and if, God forbid, we should need medical attention, we would need to try to get to Germany. The presidential debates are going on back home, but here we get only cursory summaries on the BBC and through the *International Herald Tribune.* I'm feeling left out of American life, and want to see for myself how Gore and Bush handle the debates. Tonight I feel claustrophobic, lonely, disoriented.

SUNDAY, OCTOBER 1, 2000

I am already used to streets filled with gun-toting men. KFOR and international police are everywhere, and are always heavily armed. UNMIK's international police force, CIVPOL (Civilian Police), is especially interesting. These police officers come from Pakistan, India, Kenya, Germany, the U.S., England, Canada, Nigeria, Nepal, Turkey, Italy, Tanzania, Egypt, and many other countries. They all wear the U.N. police uniform but with the badges of their own countries. The police, KFOR, the U.N. civil servants, and all the NGOs surely make Kosovo the most cosmopolitan country in the world right now. Certainly it is one of the most heavily armed.

MONDAY, OCTOBER 2, 2000

In the Cambridge School office, Zana, one of the teachers, helps me manage the temperamental Xerox machine. The vocabulary sheet we're copying has on it a photograph of a train. She stares at it a moment and says, without looking up and almost as if I'm not there, "I don't think I can ride a train again." I haven't gotten to know Zana yet, and am surprised she has said anything to me. She continues, "When my family and I were put on the train we were all so tight we didn't think we could breathe. We needed water. The babies were all crying, and an old man died after a while. His wife started to scream."

"I'm so sorry, Zana," I say. She looks at me as if recollecting where she is and what she is doing, and seems embarrassed. She finishes my pages and hands them to me with an apologetic smile.

Later, I am sitting in the school lobby waiting for the classroom to open when Fazile, one of my students, asks shyly if she can sit by me. Of course, I tell her, happy for the opportunity to get to know her. Fazile is twenty-seven and is the breadwinner for her family—her job with an insurance company must be one of the few real noninternational jobs in the city. Like most of the other students, she is solidly Kosovar middle class, wears neat fashionable clothing, and aspires to an education and a career. She has the kind of immutable face that allows you to know exactly what she looked like as a baby, and what she will look like as an old woman. She is single and lives with her parents and her younger brothers. She has a baby nephew, she says proudly, and shows me his photograph.

She can only attend about half of each class, she tells me, as that's all the time her employer will allow her. "Please do not be offended, Teacher," she says, "when I come late or leave early."

What did you do during the spring of 1999? I ask her. Did you stay in Prishtina?

Her face becomes even more serious, but I can tell she wants to talk about the war. "No, Teacher. My family and I were made to leave our home by Serb police. They tell us we die if we stay in Prishtina. They made us get on a train."

"That must have been terrible for you," I tell her.

"Yes. It was terrible. But the worst thing was that we could not find my brothers. For three months, every day, we think they are dead."

Finally, after the war ended and the Serbs were expelled, Fazile returned to Prishtina and found her younger brothers, alive. I can tell from her simple recitation that family is everything to Fazile, and that she would do anything to keep them together, happy, alive.

"We are so happy you are here, Teacher. We can learn English from an American."

"I've heard that English accents are more highly prized than American accents," I laugh.

Fazile is diplomatic. "Albanians, we like English and American accents the same. English maybe good for some things, but for business, I think American is better."

I am one of only two native English speakers in the faculty of some forty teachers. Charley, a former sheriff from Montana and now the public information officer for CIVPOL, is the other. He teaches a class during his lunch break. Each of us has more students wanting to enroll in our classes than the school will permit. "We are lucky to be in your class, Teacher," Fazile tells me today. "Thank you for coming here to teach us."

TUESDAY, OCTOBER 3, 2000

Igballe comes by this afternoon with a big bowl of pickled cabbages and a lovely rice pudding. I invite her in. She and I sit on the sofa in the front parlor and look at each other and smile, realizing we can't talk as we'd so like to do. Wouldn't it be wonderful to really talk to Igballe, to ask her about her life, to get her opinion about what's going on in Kosovo now, to tell her about my family in

America—to just chat and gossip? After a while Igballe shrugs, gets up, laughs and says, "Agim!" "Ah, *po, po,*" I say. "Yes, yes. Agim!" We have agreed that what we need is for her son, Agim, to be here to translate. Then I thank her again for the food, *"Falemnderit."* And having exhausted my Albanian vocabulary, I hug her and she leaves.

WEDNESDAY, OCTOBER 4, 2000

Today in class we study adverbs of frequency. I ask each student to write three model sentences describing habits and routines in their lives, using an adverb of frequency. I brush my teeth regularly. I take care of my little sister frequently. I rarely study. I usually play basketball after school.

They dutifully go through the exercise, but they are eager to ask me questions about America. "Who is your favorite president, Teacher?"

After thinking a moment, I tell them it's Abraham Lincoln. Most have heard of him, but they want to know why he is my favorite. "Because he had a great, generous heart," I tell them. "Because he tried to keep the United States from breaking apart. Because he ended slavery in the United States."

They want to know about slavery. "It was a dark time in America's history," I say. "Our country kept black people enslaved for hundreds of years. And even after slavery was banned, many of us treated black people badly. We discriminated against them, denied them the right to vote, to a good education, to good jobs."

"Serbs did this to us, too!" a couple of the boys exclaim. The students have seen a connection between how whites treated blacks in the United States and how Serbs treated Albanians in Kosovo in the 1990s. I ask them to tell me about it, and they take turns giving me the history. In 1989, after Milosevic revoked the autonomy Tito had granted Kosovo in 1974, most Albanians, who comprised some 90 percent of the population, were fired from government jobs, from jobs as teachers, doctors, and nurses. Only Serbs held good jobs in the '90s, they tell me; most of their parents were unemployed. (During the '80s, I've read, when the Albanian majority dominated society in Kosovo, Serbs contend that *they* were oppressed. But in the face of the students' passions, I decide not to ask about this.)

Children were segregated in the schools, the students continue, forced to use segregated toilets. The Albanian language was banned at the university, and Albanians were harassed on the streets, arrested and detained without warrants, sometimes beaten and tortured. In self-defense Albanians created a "parallel society"—a world apart from the Serb-governed world. They created their own schools in private homes, their own medical facilities, their own "shadow" government—all of which was funded by a "tax" on the Albanian diaspora. This parallel world was theirs, it was Albanian, but it was woefully inadequate. These young people grew up with a second-rate education, inadequate medical attention, unemployed parents, and the daily fears and humiliations of the "inferior race."

They ask me about race relations in America now. I answer as honestly as I can. We have come a long, long way, I tell them. We are a country that embraces diversity of all kinds. We thrive on it. But we still have racism and intolerance—and not just against blacks. We have changed the laws. But we are still trying to change our hearts.

I can see that the students don't want to think of America as imperfect. America is Shangri-La, the Promised Land. The land of jobs and opportunity and technology, of power and affluence and generosity. It is their educational and employment mecca, the place they will all go to improve their lives and the lives of their families if they get the chance. America is the crown jewel of the planet—they do not want to know the jewel is flawed. "America is our *dream!*" exclaims Genti, a bright-eyed fifteen-year-old who idolizes the L.A. Lakers.

I don't want to destroy illusions, much less dreams. But isn't it important to understand that in America we, too, do battle with bigotry, mean-spiritedness, suspicion, and greed? But that every country can—as America has—make the commitment to create a society that protects minorities, that treasures diversity, that offers equal opportunity to everyone. And that however far we fall short of our commitment, we must continue to try to achieve it, because we know it is the right thing to do?

We all have a lot to think about after class.

THURSDAY, OCTOBER 5, 2000

Tonight we go downtown to see several human rights films. Put together by local filmmakers—including "home movies" videotaped by families hiding in the mountains, suffering in the camps—the films are graphic, horrifying. They include pictures of atrocities committed in Bosnia, Croatia, and here in Kosovo. The man sitting next to me sobs as we watch.

We return home, turn on the TV, and discover that the principal architect of all this Balkan horror, Slobodan Milosevic, is out! The Yugoslavs (who are mostly Serbs) have booted him out, voting for Vojislav Kostunica as the new president of Yugoslavia. A corrupt elections commission has called for a second round of voting. We watch the BBC coverage of the huge opposition rally in front of the Yugoslav parliament building. Protesters have stormed the building and set it on fire. Milosevic is in hiding somewhere. Will he make a last stand? Will he insist on a run-off election for the presidency, even though it seems Kostunica got a clear majority? Will there be civil war? Will Milosevic and his scheming wife wind up executed as were Nicolae Ceauşescu and his wife in Romania? And most of all, is it really possible that Yugoslavs, especially the Serbs, have finally had enough of their power-mad leader who oversaw the violent destruction of Yugoslavia? We hear jubilant shouting on the streets outside our house, the celebratory firing of pistols. It must be true.

FRIDAY, OCTOBER 6, 2000

Milosevic has conceded defeat! He won't fight the election!

But there is no real euphoria here today. My students seem pleased, but are strangely subdued. "It is a good thing, Teacher," says Leutrim, one of the fifteen-year-olds. "But it does not solve the problem." Kosovo Albanians fear that international funds will now be diverted from Kosovo and be directed to Serbia, to rebuild that country. And that the Serbian people, most of whom supported Milosevic as he waged war in Croatia, Bosnia, and then Kosovo, will suddenly be seen as his victims. "There will be a great sucking sound," says one local Albanian newspaper today, "as funds and sympathy are sucked out of Kosovo and poured into Serbia." This seems, to many Kosovo Albanians, to be the scenario of yet another monstrous injustice. And so, the fall of Milosevic is seen as a mixed blessing.

And the November elections in the U.S. worry Kosovars, as well. If George Bush is elected, many fear there will be no political will at the top for "nation building" in Kosovo.

Jehona, Pam, Ed, and I sit around our dinner table tonight. Pam, formerly of Ed's office and now a court monitor in Mitrovica, says, "It will certainly happen. America will begin to see Kosovo as Europe's problem, and we will begin to pull out of here."

Jehona looks down and says in a sad, very weary voice, "Then we are lost."

SATURDAY, OCTOBER 7, 2000

Ed and I walk down Dragodan this afternoon to the black market to look for a camp stove and canisters. "Black Mart," as we immediately dub it, is a sprawling complex of ramshackle tents and tarps and stalls and lean-tos on the mud flats behind the Sports Center. It's murky in here, and spooky. Hundreds of fast-talking vendors and slow-walking buyers make passage through the narrow aisles almost impossible. Shelves, tables, and canvas floors are crammed with products from all over the Balkans, much of it pirated or smuggled. CDs, videotapes, felt slippers, jeans, radios, candles, car parts, knives, dinnerware, pots and pans, sweaters, baby clothes, tomatoes, peppers, bananas. Huge-cupped bras built like suspension bridges. Big shiny knives with the wicked curve of scimitars. My eye is caught by a two-foot-tall gold and white plastic statue of a curvaceous nude woman with a clock in her belly, a light bulb at her head, and big crystals dripping from her outstretched arms. Matching candelabra sit on each side. And, finally, we are relieved to see, under a table in a dark corner, camp stoves and canisters.

We ask Kate to dinner, secure in the knowledge that when the electricity goes out I can heat soup on our new camp stove. Kate, who has just arrived from her home in Florida, is working with Ed, heading the War Crimes section. In her office are ten volumes documenting war crimes in Kosovo—page after page of torture, rape, murder, the burning of houses, villages. She'll be involved in the investigation of some of these unspeakable crimes; she'll be talking with families of the victims. She'll be at the morgue where UNMIK holds ghastly "clothing parades" during which they display the clothing worn by victims in the hope that some families can identify their loved ones. Hundreds of bodies remain in the morgue, unidentified, unburied. Ed tells Kate of an UNMIK employee he met last week who, having seen baby shoes in the clothing parade, cannot bear to return.

Kate is tough. She was a public defender doing death penalty cases in Florida. And she has a heart full of concern, compassion. She wants to help. But is she, is anyone, ready for this?

MONDAY, OCTOBER 9, 2000

I am in love with my students. They are bright, fun, curious, receptive. Today they practice speaking, repeating each sentence after me in perfect imitation, and I realize with chagrin that these Kosovo Albanian students are being taught to speak English not only with an American accent, but with a *southern* accent! It seems that, even after twenty-one years in California, my southern drawl is still with me—and now, with my students!

We're having so much fun that I wonder, perversely, if they could possibly be learning anything.

TUESDAY, OCTOBER 10, 2000

It is maddening to hear commentators and pundits on the BBC talking of the "valiant" Serbian people who have so "courageously" overthrown their "tyrant," Slobodan Milosevic. The Serbs are being spoken of as Milosevic's "victims," when the fact is that many of them *voted* for Milosevic again and again. Yes, he was a tyrant who cynically manipulated both elections and Serb nationalism and ethnic prejudices to increase his own power. And, yes, there was always an opposition, students and others, who loathed Milosevic and his politics of racial hatred. But it seems to me that it was not his *waging* wars that angered most Serbs—it was his *losing* wars. And the revolution didn't come until he was accused of stealing from *them,* from the Serb nation. It was the charges of embezzlement and financial mismanagement of the Serb nation that finally brought him down. Many Serbs bought his act for a long time.

I keep hearing in the Western press that Kosovo has been wracked by ethnic struggle for a thousand years. A kind of international shrug: "Oh, well. They've always killed each other in Kosovo. What can you do?" But it's not that simple. We discuss this with friends from OSCE tonight at dinner. For most of their history, Serbs and Albanians lived relatively peaceably with each other, Ed argues. Not without tension and conflicts, but no more than between the French and the Germans, for example, or for that matter between rival Christian sects in many parts of Europe. What changed, Ed says, is that in the last hundred years or so unscrupulous nationalist leaders capitalized on all the myths, prejudices, and jealousies, stirred up the embers of ethnic passions and created deadly new hatreds. Milosevic's vicious ten-year propaganda campaign against Kosovo Albanians brought out the worst in the Serbian population, and is largely responsible for the devastation of both Kosovo and Serbia proper.

So, we wonder, maybe if, after all, they haven't *always* killed each other, might Albanians and Serbs, with different leadership, be able to live together again? Might progressive, tolerant leadership bring out the *best* in people?

In any case, we in the rest of the world cannot so easily dismiss the Balkan problem as being ancient and thus intractable. We cannot so easily shrug off our responsibility to help.

WEDNESDAY, OCTOBER 11, 2000

Leonard. The name is not pronounced as we pronounce it. It requires a serious curling of the mouth around the "L" and a gurgle in the back of the throat that I have not yet mastered. Leonard is one of my students, and the first one to take me up on my offer to help with any special English-language needs. He came up to me after class today to say he wants to apply for a Soros Foundation scholarship to study at the American University in Bulgaria—AUBG. He is eighteen, and will finish high school next spring. There are two things, he says, he needs my help with right away. Could I write a recommendation for him? And could I help him with the essay, an essential part of the application, in which he is to describe why he wants to go to AUBG. Then, after next week, when his application must be submitted to the foundation, he would like my help studying for the TOEFL, the Test of English as a Foreign Language. He must pass this test and the SAT (Scholastic Aptitude Test) to attend the university.

I have gotten to know Leonard a bit. He is a quiet, serious young man who rarely speaks in class, but who listens with an extraordinary intensity. When he smiles, he lowers his head and opens his mouth only a fraction to hide his slightly prominent front teeth. Both the size and the sweetness of his large brown eyes are magnified by his thick glasses. He is slender and angular but he is not at all awkward. His walk and his gestures are graceful, delicate almost, and his voice is soft and filled with a gentleness I could not begin to describe.

I also know something of his war story. A couple of weeks ago I asked him if he left Prishtina on the infamous trains, spending the rest of the war in the refugee camps as most of his countrymen did. "No, Teacher," he said. "My family stayed in our apartment. We hid from the soldiers and the police. It was . . . ," he gropes for the word, "a prison. And we were prisoners." They had no car to use for escape, and somehow the paramilitaries never came to their apartment to roust them out to the trains. They spent the war in hiding in a low-rise building in the center of the city. His mother would go out each day to find food for the family. Leonard and his father dared not leave the apartment lest they be captured and killed as potential KLA fighters, so, with Leonard's nine-year-old sister and his mother, they huddled in their tiny flat for three months.

Leonard's world outside the flat, he says, was what he could see through a hole in the curtain. "Sometimes the Serbian police came," Leonard says. "Some of them knew we were here. They would knock on the door and say they will take me, and my mother would give them money and they would go away."

"Leonard, you must all have been terrified."

Leonard's soft voice is always hesitant as he searches for English words. Now it is even more hesitant, for he hasn't the vocabulary to describe what they felt. But he sums it up well when he says, "Every day my family is scared, Teacher. Every day we think we will die."

I ask him if he heard the NATO bombing. "Ah, yes, of course." Leonard has a way of pursing his lips to indicate that something is self-evident. "One night my sister and I were sleeping by the window. A bomb drops and our building shakes and the window breaks into many pieces and falls on us. We are lucky that we have pulled up . . ." "The covers," I fill in. "Yes. And so the covers saved us." Incredibly, he smiles at this. "We had much lucky, I think.

"And we knew that these bombs were a good thing," he continues. "These bombs were our friends.

The day of the "liberation," as Leonard puts it, he went outside and met a "strange city," a "place I hadn't seen before. Prishtina was new to me that day. For the first time in many years I could walk on the street and not be afraid."

Today he is a young man on a mission. "Teacher," he says. "This is my chance. Albanian students, we must leave Kosova for our education so we can provide for our families here. I want to study computers, and here, in my school, we have no computers. We learn theory only. We must have equipment. I know American universities have the best; they have everything we need to learn. And I will work very hard so they will accept me."

My students—seventeen young men and women now, mostly in their teens, three of them in their twenties or thirties—have told me about the educational system here. First, a Communist system where textbooks were dull, discipline was strict, and as each student confirms to me, "You were not allowed to have opinions." Then, when Milosevic cracked down on Kosovo Albanians in 1989, most of these young people started attending classes held in homes where, they told me, "your lap became your desk." Police often raided these homes, breaking up the classes and occasionally arresting and beating the teachers. "Police shot tear gas into our classroom," twenty-four-year-old Emina told me, "and took my teacher outside to beat him up. But we didn't let them win. We kept going to our school, our teacher kept teaching us." Books were scarce, equipment of any kind nonexistent. Their education, needless to say, suffered for years. What they want now, more than anything else, is a chance to study abroad. Their future, and more important to them, the future of their families, depends on it.

And so, Leonard thinks, this will now be his chance to leave Kosovo for an education in an American university. To do this he must pass the TOEFL in January, only two months from now.

I hesitate. "Leonard, these are very difficult tests. You have to have a very high level of English to pass. Most students in other parts of the world study for many months, take special courses to learn how to take the test . . ."

"Teacher," he says, "I am optimist. I will work very hard and, I am sure, if I work hard I will have success." Where does he get this incredible optimism? Nothing in his personal history, or his country's history, justifies it.

Yet this is what I see everywhere here in Prishtina. Optimism, energy, the belief that things will be better, that there is a future and that that future is bright, bountiful even. My students are smart, full of enthusiasm, fun-loving, hardworking. But behind each eager, smiling face lies a hidden memory of grief, terror, loss. Everyone here has been wounded. How is it they can appear so hopeful, so happy?

As Leonard looks at me, waiting for my answer, I hope he can't tell how worried I am. I have no idea what to say to him. I must be so careful. I don't want to discourage him. How could I? But he is starting so late, and the odds are stacked so high against him. If I encourage him and he fails the test, will he lose hope about his future? What should I do?

I can say I will help him. Of course. We will work together and do our best. Leonard is very happy with this. "Oh!" he says, and I fear he is about to cry. "Thank you, Teacher! I will work very hard. Thank you, Teacher!"

THURSDAY, OCTOBER 12, 2000

My walk to school today:

Out onto the street of cut stones in front of our house to first greet the neighbors across the street, the man and his two teenaged sons who are always working on their car in the morning. *"Mire dita!"* I call to them, and they bring their heads up out of the engine, waving wrenches and screwdrivers in greeting. I wave to neighbor women out hanging clothes or sweeping their porches; they smile and call out, *"Mire dita!"* Past Orhan, the shopkeeper, who is putting out the morning edition of *Koha Ditore,* and along our street already clamorous with the sounds of hammers and electric drills, avoiding potholes and tottering piles of brick and lumber and ducking under dangerously drooping electrical wires. Further along, graffiti tagged on bare concrete walls: LDK, PDK, AAK, KLA, *"Fuck the Rules!"* Death notices with photographs of the deceased are stapled to doors and telephone posts. Down the crumbling concrete steps, on either side of the midden that is Dragodan, years or decades of refuse spilling down the bare slopes. Past a chicken coop and down to the flats where the train tracks parallel the road circling the hill. I negotiate the broad expanse of mud and standing water and piles of smoldering garbage along the disused tracks. No trains have run here since the trains that carried terrified Albanians to the camps at the border. I arrive at one of the major intersections of downtown. The traffic lights don't work, of course. A tractor pulling a wagon-load of red roof tiles, a KFOR tank, and a dozen shabby cars and trucks negotiate the crossroads in the proven local manner: First, crowd together all at once into the center, creating as much havoc as possible. *Then* begin to figure out a plan of disentanglement. Kosovars can't avoid getting into these traffic snarls, but they are good at getting out of them. I zigzag around several vehicles, holding my breath to avoid their noxious fumes, and find the dirt road that takes me to the soccer stadium, its outer walls lined with merchants' stalls. Across from the stadium sit the bombed hulks of the Serb police complex. The outer walls have gone, exposing five levels of charred ceilings/floors collapsed in diagonals on top of each other. The giant radio tower that was central to Serb communications sprawls broken on the mud, still pinning the Volkswagen it fell on in March 1999 when NATO bombs dropped.

Then to the lower level of the Sports Center complex that houses the Cambridge School, through the murky maze of shops and restaurants where I buy an orange Fanta to take with me into class. And then up to the large concrete plaza, empty today, so a student tells me, because the police are trying to rid the area of drug dealers. Then into the Sports Center lobby, damp and dark and musty, and up the stairs to school . . . where the young staff greet me with a cheerful "Hello, Paula!" And into my classroom where the students who have come for special tutoring await me.

Friday, October 13, 2000

After school it is drizzling rain, so I hail a cab. A moment after I get in, a man gets in the front seat, apparently a friend of the driver. If any other guy gets in, I decide, I'm outta here. The cabbie swings wildly around the Sports Center complex and heads for Dragodan the back way, through the black market. He looks back at me and asks *"Deutsch?"* "No," I say, "American. San Francisco." "Ah!" he gesticulates happily, both hands off the wheel, pointing to his chest. "Detroit, me! Two years!" By this time we all realize we are stuck in a traffic jam in the black market. A car ahead of us has somehow positioned itself perpendicular to the street, blocking both lanes of traffic. Horns blare up and down the street. From time to time my driver leans on his horn, simply to pass the time. Not three feet away on either side sit the black market vendors on their tarps on the mud or at their tables. Bed linens in plastic wrappers, pocket knives and bright plastic flowers, plastic buckets and cartons of cigarettes, bananas, candy bars, potatoes. And in the mud and the street, the refuse of all these products: candy bar wrappers, banana peels, cigarette butts, rotting vegetables. After a few minutes the other passenger hops out, goes to a stall and returns with a big bunch of bananas. He hands one to the driver, one to me, and we sit munching our bananas surrounded by the bedlam of the black market waiting for someone up front to move. And eventually, of course, someone does.

SATURDAY, OCTOBER 14, 2000

Ed and I drive north out of town today to look around. In only a short while we see KFOR signs warning that we are about to leave Kosovo, to enter Serbia. Can't do that, of course, so we turn around. The countryside here is bleak, colorless, the small towns and farmhouses poor, run-down even when not war-damaged. Like the rest of Kosovo, this area was "cleansed," starting in 1998 and accelerating in the spring of 1999. The cleansing was quick and efficient, for by the time Serbs turned their attention to Kosovo, they had already perfected the methods of ethnic cleansing in Bosnia. The Yugoslav army, and even more, Serb gangster-paramilitaries, knew what to do: First, shell or throw grenades into the village to announce your presence; then force everyone out onto the street and separate the men and adolescent boys from the women and children; kill some, rape some, terrorize the rest; loot homes and businesses, keeping some of the money and goods for yourself, saving the rest to send back to Belgrade; destroy homes and barns and livestock; transport women, children, and old people to the borders or make them walk, confiscate their identity and ownership papers so they can't return, then kick them out of the country. And, in many cases, kill the men and boys you've kept behind. A fast, effective plan to rid Bosnia of Bosnian Muslims, and Kosovo of Albanians. In a matter of weeks Serbian forces were able to roust 90 percent of all ethnic Albanians from their homes, some 1.3 million, expelling some 860,000 people from the country, and internally displacing the rest. In that short period, they were able to severely damage or destroy nearly half of all Albanian homes.

As we drive through the ruined towns and villages, the devastated countryside with its blackened barns, its shell-blasted trees, it is easy to imagine the scenes in the streets as husbands and fathers were separated from their families, as long lines of refugees snaked through the hills seeking safety. It is a tragic, eloquent landscape.

This evening at home, we hear gunshots, lots of them, echoing through the final calls to prayer from the mosques downtown.

MONDAY, OCTOBER 16, 2000

Luan is a thirty-year-old mechanical engineer. He works as an assistant in the university's faculty of mechanical engineering and spends part of his time in my class, thinking English might be a passport to further education out of the country. He has black eyes and his hair, also black, is beginning to recede. His face is slightly pockmarked and his voice raspy. His English is poor—he often can't keep up with the rest of the class, and sometimes the teenagers laugh at his halting attempts to pronounce difficult words. Yet, he laughs with them, and is unfailingly courteous, even shyly affectionate, to me. I am already immensely fond of him.

Surprisingly for so rough-looking a young man, he is also a published poet who admires Carl Sandburg. Today he brings me a small volume in which fifteen of the poems are his own. He has autographed it, "To my teacher, Paula, with great respect. Luan." He points to his two favorite poems and tells me he wrote them before the war. "I cannot write poetry now, not about the war. It is too soon. Maybe in a few years." He shrugs and manages a smile.

After class, Leonard and his friend Ardi ask me, with formal courtesy, if they can have the pleasure of buying me a coffee. I can see that Leonard wants to do something to thank me for agreeing to help him. So we go to the Monaco Café below the school where we chat together and drink macchiato. What dear young men.

TUESDAY, OCTOBER 17, 2000

The application is in. I meet Leonard downtown today and we put the pieces together, then he walks to the Soros Foundation office to turn it in. Leonard had written an essay in English, which I reviewed over the weekend, correcting grammar, suggesting structural changes, but making sure Leonard's passionate longing for a good education comes through loud and clear. In my recommendation I pointed out that somehow this young man, a straight-A student, had had the strength of character to emerge from the terrors of war with hope for the future and a dream of an American education. Surely this is the kind of student who should be encouraged with financial aid. Without it, he hasn't a chance. His father, a primary school geography teacher and the sole breadwinner, earns about $130 a month.

Please, Soros Foundation, give him a chance.

WEDNESDAY, OCTOBER 18, 2000

I have found a TOEFL preparation book! The Dukagjini bookstore on Mother Teresa Boulevard, the only bookstore in town with books in English, had a lone copy of the Cambridge Preparation for the TOEFL. A miracle! I snapped it up quickly. The only one in the city; I'm sure the only one in the country. I give it to Leonard after class and tell him we can structure our studies around the text. We will meet after each class and tackle some new aspect of the language. Leonard is thrilled. He hadn't expected such luck. And we agree we'll make the book available to others who need it, as well.

But he really needs a TOEFL preparation class, the kind that teaches not only the grammar but also the "tricks" of the test. I can't help Leonard with that, and though I've asked about it all over town, it seems no one is teaching such a course. The odds against Leonard remain impossibly high.

In class we have a listening lesson. As always the tape is scratchy, barely audible, but I see several students look uneasy as the narrator speaks of a work of art that "even God couldn't have created so beautifully." When I ask for response to the reading, Emina, a bright twenty-four-year-old with short, curly black hair and Elizabeth Taylor eyes who joined the class a couple of weeks ago, quickly raises her hand. "Teacher," she says, "I do not like where the man says God cannot create something this good. No one can make things like God does! This man shows great disrespect for God and I think it is wrong!" Others nod in agreement. "But I want you to know, Teacher," she continues, "that I do not care if this man has my religion. We are mostly Muslims here, but not all people need to be Muslims. Many religions are good. It is important only to love God."

Albanians, at least here in Prishtina, do not wear their religion on their sleeves. Islam here seems to be, well, "easygoing" is the word that comes to mind. Their religion is important. They go to the mosque, they celebrate Ramadan, they speak of God with love and respect. But unlike many Muslim countries around the world that are crippled by religious fanaticism, Kosovo is a secular society. Even Kosovars' complaints against the Serbs seem not to stem from, or even to be fed by, their religion.

"You love God, don't you, Teacher?" Emina asks anxiously. It's a tricky question for me, having settled long ago on the idea of God as simply "a big mystery." But I look at these sweet, trusting, hopeful young faces before me and think, "If this isn't God, what is?" So I answer, "Yes, Emina, I love God."

THURSDAY, OCTOBER 19, 2000

Work on a lesson plan about adverbs, wash clothes and hang them out, walk downtown where I buy ingredients for tonight's dinner and e-mail Mama and Daddy, son Paul and stepsons Paul and Brian. I reassure everyone that we are safe, that we are happy.

Then back up Dragodan to Ed's office where I encounter a young woman who wants ABA-CEELI to get involved with women's issues. "Women barely exist as human beings in Kosova," she declares. "Someone needs to give them courage to *demand* their rights."

Dafina goes on to explain that she just met with a young woman, a refugee from the countryside, whose husband was killed in the war and who now lives with her in-laws and baby son in a squalid garage flat here in Prishtina. "The husband's parents feel their daughter-in-law is a burden. They want her to leave. But she must leave the baby with them." The in-laws' position is consistent with ancient custom as articulated in the Kanun of Lek, still widely adhered to in some rural areas. A widow, according to this traditional standard, may remarry, but children of the dead son belong to that son's male relatives.

Women have immense burdens in Kosovo, Dafina contends, but few rights and protections, particularly in these remote mountain areas where primitive ideas that have virtually disappeared from the rest of Europe still dominate village life.

There are, she says, strong, active women's organizations in Kosovo that seek to improve the lives of women. Most of these groups were created as a response to the Serb oppression of the '90s, and are headed by dynamic women lawyers, doctors, and human rights activists. But the international community must become more involved, Dafina argues, if women in Kosovo are to have a chance. She complains that UNMIK and OSCE are not doing enough for women here.

Tonight, lying in bed writing my journal, I think of the young woman and her baby, virtually imprisoned by her in-laws in a flat not too far from ours. Was Dafina able to give her the right kind of advice today, show her a way to reclaim her life? Dafina was not optimistic about the young woman's chances of breaking free. Tradition can be the cruelest prison of all.

FRIDAY, OCTOBER 20, 2000

The Prishtina Sports Center dominates the city. Built in the 1960s, it was Tito's bribe to Kosovars, his version of bread and circuses. A huge Communist-Futurist–style complex, the center burned right after the war. Rumors abound about arson, but everyone agrees that the fire wasn't put out in time because the city was still in a state of anarchy—no one knew who was in charge of firefighting. And so it looms over the city now, a dark specter, its charred beams and twisted, melted frame looking like some gigantic space station crash-landed in the middle of the city.

I work here, in a corner of this massive ruin that the Cambridge School recently carved out for itself. Glass windows remain broken, exposing the hallway to the elements. My classroom smells of smoke. We have no video, no computers, no library, and the audiotape player is usually broken. Many of my students learn from copies of copies of textbooks. I teach in my coat and wool hat and gloves, for there is no heat, and when the electricity goes off, I teach in the dark. Yet I love this place and the people in it. The staff are unfailingly courteous as they struggle to learn how to run a school. And the students . . . well, I love each one of these seventeen young people. I am awed by their courage, by their spirit.

Leonard arrives at school today looking tired and blue, circles under his eyes. His smile, still sweet, is forced. Finally, with coaxing, "I didn't sleep last night, Teacher. I looked at the TOEFL book." Uh, oh. "Usually I am optimist, Teacher, but this TOEFL, this is very, very hard, I think." I can tell he has been overwhelmed by this big, thick book, and has suddenly realized the immensity of his undertaking.

And so we talk. Finally I tell him, "Leonard, you may pass the test the first time you take it. Or, like many students, you may have to take it many times before you pass it. You are young. You have time. Meanwhile, the main thing is that you don't jeopardize your health trying to keep your grades up, studying for the TOEFL, taking this English class. You must sleep, you must eat. You must stop worrying. It will be all right." I went on like this for a while and he began to perk up. He said, "Teacher, I am feeling better now. Your words make me feel better." And he goes home, promising me he will go to bed early and get some sleep.

Words. The power they have. They can heal and encourage, but they can do such damage. My students listen carefully to everything I say, and believe that, because I am an American in Kosovo, helping them, I am both knowledgeable and wise. Their faith in me is frightening. I do so want to say the right things, do the right things. But I feel so inadequate, *am* so inadequate. At least tonight I can believe that I said the right words to help Leonard get a good night's sleep. It is something.

SATURDAY, OCTOBER 21, 2000

Last week, the Cambridge School asked me to proof an essay written by a young man who is trying to get into a summer study program in the U.S. Among other things this young man spoke of his love and admiration for his father, a prominent pacifist political leader. Today I learn that this boy's father was gunned down in front of his apartment yesterday, the victim, it is thought, of a political assassination, either by Serbs or by rival Albanian factions. I am sickened at the news, at the awful irony of a pacifist leader suffering a violent death.

Tonight Ed and I discuss once again the nature of evil. "Almost no one sets out to do something 'evil,'" Ed says. "They don't say to themselves, consciously at least, 'Today I'm going to commit an evil act.' They say, 'I'm going to kill this person so my people will be free,' or 'I'm going to burn these houses so my country can be safe,' or 'I'm going to murder these people because they did terrible things to my people.' Evil is attributed to the victim, and so, evil acts can be justified by the perpetrator as good. Maybe later some few perpetrators say, My God, what have I done? But only a few. It is never simple." I love Ed's thoughtfulness, his willingness to try to understand, even when he can't condone. And it's so *hard* to understand anything here.

MONDAY, OCTOBER 23, 2000

The students and I have formed The Hemingway Book Club of Kosova. Last week I found a copy of Hemingway's *The Old Man and the Sea*—probably the only one in the country—and had copies of it made for everyone in the class. It's the right length, the prose is simple enough for the intermediate level, and its story, I think, will resonate with these brave young people. I'll have to be alert for Hemingway's macho, though. God knows this country doesn't need any more macho.

I put together from the web a logo with the name of our club and a wonderful drawing of a marlin. I hand it out today to much admiration, and one reservation they all share: "Teacher, you have spelled it 'Kosovo'. That is wrong. It should be 'Kosova.'" Kosova, with an "a," is the Albanian form of the word, and is a political statement. The U.N. doesn't want "Kosova" used because it connotes independence from Serbia. But this book club belongs to these Albanian students. I will change it to Kosova.

Today I give everyone their books and the first set of "focus questions"—things to think about as they read the first twenty pages. Then, on November 11, a Saturday, those who want can come to our house for the first club meeting. Everyone seems to be excited about it. It is, they say, the first book in English they've owned. For some, it is their first book in any language other than texts they use at school.

After class Leonard comes up to me. I can tell he has something especially serious to say, even for so serious a young man. "Teacher." He hesitates, ill at ease with both language and circumstance. "I want to tell you . . . we cannot believe anyone would be so kind to us. You encourage, you spend time with us. You give us the books. No one else does this for us ever." I start to say something, but

Leonard keeps going. "I want you to know that you are special, Teacher. And, I don't . . . compliment you . . . no, that is not the right word." "Flatter," I offer. "Yes, flatter. I don't flatter you. I only tell you the truth."

I struggle not to cry as I realize, for the first time really, how true it is that Leonard and his classmates have not been able to depend upon the kindness of strangers. For much of their lives they and their Albanian countrymen have been the victims of a vicious apartheid that imprisoned them in poverty, in ignorance, in a world where the only kindness came from their own Albanian community, and not always then. They were mistreated by their Serb masters and ignored by the rest of us. Now, suddenly, after the war, the massacres, the ethnic cleansing, there are people here helping them. Helping them rebuild their homes and roads, helping them write laws and develop a legal system, and here I am, at the Cambridge School, helping some of them learn English, gain access to the wider world. I offer only the most ordinary brand of human kindness, but here, to these students, that ordinary kindness seems a miracle.

WEDNESDAY, OCTOBER 25, 2000

A couple of months before coming here, I was driving along the beautiful Bolinas lagoon not far from our house, half-listening to NPR when the word "Kosovo" arrested my attention. I pulled off the side of the road to give my full attention to the interview. The woman being interviewed was Dr. Vjosa Dobruna. She and her colleague, Sevdie Ahmeti, founded the Center for the Protection of Women and Children in Kosovo. Both Dr. Dobruna and Ms. Ahmeti have been recognized by international human rights organizations for their work with victimized and oppressed Kosovar women and children. I resolved that day to visit the center when we got to Prishtina.

So today Ed and I visit Ms. Ahmeti, who is directing the center now, in the unprepossessing storefront center on Sunny Hill. Without her e-mail address, with no mail, and with no landline phones here, we have come without an appointment. We knock on the open door to her office and introduce ourselves. She graciously invites us to call her Sevdie and asks us to be seated. An assistant brings us glasses of juice and coffee—Kosovars unfailingly offer gracious old-world hospitality—and the other assistants disappear and shut the door behind them.

We have heard about the center, Ed says, and have come to see if there's something we can do to help—in particular, if there's some way the American Bar Association's program here can assist. Sevdie takes this introduction for what it is: an invitation to tell us about her work.

Long before the 1998–99 war, Sevdie and Dr. Dobruna worked with rape and domestic violence victims, and advocated for human rights of Albanians in Kosovo. For their efforts both were jailed several times. Sevdie says she was stripped, tortured, and beaten on several occasions. When the war started she was high on the Serbs' most-wanted list. One day masked paramilitaries broke into the house where she was hiding and tortured Sevdie, her husband, and brother-in-law. She was "humiliated," as she puts it, with the barrel of a rifle. (I know that she bravely told of her ordeal right after the war in an effort to encourage other rape victims to seek help.) But she survived, remaining in Kosovo throughout the war, continuing to help and counsel victims even while in hiding.

It was what was done to women during the Serb aggression of 1998–99 that she wants to talk about. Thirty thousand rapes of Albanian girls and women by Serb forces, she claims. Official figures mean nothing because few women will admit to rape, and even fewer relatives will admit their daughter/wife/mother/sister was a rape victim. The husband or father, Sevdie says with disgust, "see rape as a crime against *their* honor. They deny their daughter or wife even their status as victim, appropriating that role to themselves."

So in reality many women and girls were victimized twice: first by their Serb rapists, and second by their own families, who often ostracized them because they had, through their rape, brought dishonor on the family. The women she counsels, then, have frequently been cast off from their families and have no place to go. In the eyes of their families, their society—indeed, in their own eyes—they have become nonpersons. They are ruined forever. They live in fear and despair, poverty and degradation. They suffer frequent flashbacks.

Sevdie is a tall, sturdily built, handsome woman with close-cropped gray hair, intense blue eyes, and a deep, commanding voice. She is wearing slim wool trousers pulled down over leather boots, and a patterned scarf at her neck. She is intense, passionate, outraged, sorrowful. She never loses eye contact with us.

She goes to her file cabinet and pulls out some pictures taken at a village she visited last month. The first is of an old woman whose only son was killed and whose many daughters were raped in front of her. "Look at her face!" Sevdie urges. The next picture is of a group of village women—old and young—gathered together in a room. Most of these women, Sevdie says, were raped, and are just now willing to talk about it. It is talking together—weeping, raging together—that is the best treatment, she says. "Look at their faces." She points to face after face. "Look at their faces!" Sevdie would will us to see what she has seen, know what she knows.

Before and during the war, she tells us, Serb paramilitary and police used the basement of the economics faculty at the university as a rape chamber. Dozens of young women were taken here and repeatedly raped by Serbs while their drunken compatriots watched and cheered. After the war Sevdie found women's bras and panties in the room, some torn and bloody, liquor bottles and empty cigarette packs lining the walls where the spectators sat, and graffiti everywhere, including one sign that said: "Frustrated? Take it out between a woman's legs." Many of the women who disappeared into this and other "rape camps" never reappeared.

In the refugee camps those known to be rape victims were asked to give their stories to U.N. officials, and later, after returning to their homes, to fill out endless forms, to give interviews to still more officials. Then . . . nothing. No help, no counseling, no protection, no job training. It is this gap that Sevdie's small organization tries to fill.

Not all of Sevdie's work is war-related. From another file she takes out a page with several color pictures pasted to it. It is a lovely young girl whose face is suffused with terror and despair, angry red wounds marring her face and chest. Recently she was raped by men in her village, and, after bravely reporting the rape, was abducted by her rapists' families and friends, raped again, and tortured. "Look at her face!" Sevdie says again, and we see the awful burns on the innocent skin. The young woman testified in court about all this but recanted after being held by the carabinieri, the Italian police (part of the UNMIK international police force), who, Sevdie implies, allowed her to be intimidated throughout the trial. The girl apologized to Sevdie for her "weakness," then disappeared. The new legal system here has failed this poor young woman completely. Sevdie is trying to find her, find out if she is all right.

"But I can no longer bear to listen to the stories as I used to do," Sevdie says with a sigh. "I have listened too long."

After we leave I know that, because I don't speak Albanian, there is not much practical assistance I can provide Sevdie. But I can see that Ed is already trying to come up with ways his organization might try to help.

FRIDAY, OCTOBER 27, 2000

Things are heating up here. In the last week or so gunfire has increased—the crackle of shots down the hill, the resounding *bam* of a rifle down the street. Many times, all day, into the evening. Sheryl and Kate, the American attorneys who've arrived to work with Ed, report that a bomb exploded right next to their apartment last night—some Albanians blowing up a Serb-owned building. We heard the explosion all the way up here on Dragodan. KFOR troops and international police are thick on the ground—maybe four or five times the number usually out on the streets. And they are alert, watchful.

The reason: the first democratic elections will be held in Kosovo this weekend, Saturday, and although the elections themselves are for municipal offices only, every Kosovo Albanian sees these elections as a referendum on who will lead them to independence. By voting for their party's candidates for local offices—there are three main parties—they are really saying whom they want as president of an independent Kosovo. And just by voting, they are saying strongly and clearly that they will have nothing to do with Serbia ever again, that they are autonomous.

This is inaccurate, of course. The U.N. maintains that Kosovo is still part of Serbia and will one day be reintegrated. Before the Yugoslav elections, that idea seemed merely a convenient fiction. But now that Kostunica is president of Yugoslavia, and Europe and America are showering him with money and affiliations, Kosovo Albanians are very nervous. Will there be any support, anywhere in the world, for their independence now that the monster, Milosevic, is gone? Will they, after all, become part of Serbia, of Yugoslavia, again?

A local newspaper says the difference between Kostunica and Milosevic is the difference between Coke and Pepsi. All Serbs are murderous toward Kosovo Albanians. So, no! They will never again be part of Serbia! With these elections they stake their claim in the world of nations.

And so the atmosphere around these elections, already intense, has been made electrical. The ultra-nationalist Kostunica added voltage this week when he asked the U.N. to postpone these elections in Kosovo, and, with the support of Putin in Russia, proclaimed again Serbia's ownership of Kosovo.

We're on "black alert," two notches down from "red." The U.S. Mission here has warned all American nationals to be extremely vigilant, and has asked us not to leave our homes this weekend. We've had to register for possible evacuation. Some NGOs have already evacuated, and the U.S. Mission debated whether to evacuate all of us. Decided against it.

The fear is on several levels: Kosovo Serbs, furious about Kosovo elections, may plant bombs, shoot people, and in general try to disrupt the elections. They might specifically target Americans. Or competing factions of Kosovo Albanians might express their differences in bullets rather than words, and Americans might get caught in the cross fire.

I was downtown this week when two political rallies were going on. The first, on Wednesday, was for the leading candidate's party. Ibrahim Rugova has been the de facto leader of Kosovo for ten years, and is a mild-mannered professorial pacifist. During the ten years of apartheid, Rugova led his country in passive resistance and in creating the "parallel" institutions, causing some to call him the "Gandhi of Kosovo." But his pacifism didn't work. Other nations, including the U.S., failed to offer Rugova adequate support, and Serb oppression of the Albanian majority in Kosovo only grew worse through the years. Rugova's rally this week, though huge, was relatively sedate. I stood outside the soccer stadium watching the crowd come out, waving Albanian flags, and sometimes, strangely, American flags attached to Albanian flags. (UNMIK has issued a rule that the Albanian flag not be shown or flown during the elections. Too provocative, they say. But no one pays any attention.)

Then Thursday, Ed and I stood on the balcony of his office at the top of Dragodan listening to the sounds of the second rally. The speakers' passionate voices, the chants, the cheers, the roar of thirty thousand people boomed up to us from the stadium downtown. "Strange how from this position democracy sounds just like fascism," Ed said. This was the PDK, the party headed by Hashim Thaci, a handsome, dashing, former Kosova Liberation Army leader. It was this guerrilla group that surfaced in the late '90s after it became clear that Rugova's civil disobedience would neither win the world's support nor make the Serbs back off. The KLA started attacking Serb police and security forces (and, it is said, sometimes Albanian collaborators), quickly growing larger and more effective. I walked down from Dragodan to see this rally close up. This crowd seemed rougher, more intense. Thousands and thousands of young men, traveling in packs as they left the stadium, with fierce eyes and grim, determined mouths. And everywhere the blood-red flag with its black double-headed eagle.

When I came home, Agim, our landlord's son, was in the yard smoking a cigarette. I asked him if he had been to the rally. No, he was going to vote for Ramush Haradinaj's party, the AAK. Haradinaj is a former KLA leader, too, he said. "What are his plans for building a strong country, a better country?" I asked him. Agim looked blank. "I don't know." "Then why are you going to vote for his party?" "Haradinaj was a brave fighter! And two of his brothers were killed by Serbs in the war!" I waited for more. But that was it. Agim's explanation of why he supports the AAK. It is enough for

Agim, and, I expect, for thousands more like him who will give their support to the former guerrilla hero.

We are watching a people struggle to build a nation, to win independence. It is exciting, it is intriguing, but above all it is sad. Kosovo is so poor. No manufacturing, little commerce, a poor educational system, no money, no infrastructure. Just an overwhelming desire for a national identity, to be free of persecution.

And to be free to persecute? Agim, and many others like him, would say yes. They have no intention of tolerating Serbs in Kosovo ever again. Or for that matter, Roma (Gypsies), Gorani, or any of the other minorities that made Kosovo such a culturally rich and diverse country not long ago. Most of these minorities are now suspected of possible collaboration with the Serbs. So, many here want a purely Albanian Kosovo. Period.

SATURDAY, OCTOBER 28, 2000, ELECTION DAY

We decide we can't stay cooped up in the house, in spite of official warnings not to go out today. So we get in the Jeep and, at the end of our street, are stopped by coils of razor wire and a tank, KFOR troops guarding the U.S. Mission. Ed shows them his badge and they let us through. Coming back from his office we run into another such road block. But we see no indication of violence, and nothing is reported on our local internet sources. A peaceful election after all.

Ed and I are thinking tonight about a long weekend in Istanbul, despite a state department warning that a terrorist group headed by Osama bin Laden might be planning attacks against Americans in Turkey. But we're not worried. After all, we're living in Kosovo. How much more dangerous could an Arab terrorist be?

SUNDAY, OCTOBER 29, 2000

I am in the upstairs parlor working on my lesson plan. Isa, our landlord, is here with me, jerry-rigging the wiring to support a new
emergency generator. Suddenly, a loud knocking on the door, an in-
sistent ringing of the doorbell. I run downstairs to find a neighbor
who tells me, "You must move your car!" and he points in the direction of the street. There, stuck behind our Jeep Cherokee, is a
huge armored personnel carrier, a helmeted soldier sticking his
head up through the hatch, the big gun on its turret pointed down
the street. Several more military vehicles are lined up behind it. Soldiers stand around surveying the situation, looking intently at the
rear bumper of the Jeep sticking out into the road. Oh, no. "I have
no key," I tell our neighbor. "My husband is gone. He has the only
key." He shrugs but looks worried. I can only return upstairs. Isa
and I look out the window at the scene below. Our little Jeep holding up the might of KFOR. I start to feel a bit anxious. Then Isa
and I look at each other, unable to communicate a word, and both
burst out laughing! I decide not to watch whatever happens on the
street, and when I look again an hour later, the street is cleared, our
Jeep still intact. Amazing how some problems disappear when you
ignore them.

MONDAY, OCTOBER 30, 2000

After class Leonard and his friend Ardi are pumped up about the
election last Saturday. (Rugova's LDK party won two thirds of the
municipalities, a victory for moderates.) They both had jobs assist-
ing at one of the polling places, and though they are too young to

vote, they have strong opinions on the candidates. Having supported different parties, they tease each other. Winner! Loser! But they know that they *both* won on Saturday. The whole country won. They describe the excitement in the polling places, the lines stretching back many blocks, old people in wheelchairs, the war-wounded on crutches, the young mothers with babies in arms. Thousands of voters waiting patiently for hours to get their first chance to cast a free ballot.

"And isn't it great," I say, looking at the boys' flushed young faces, "that in a democracy you can disagree and still be friends?" The two losing party leaders have yielded gracefully, promising to support the winning party. Let's hope it stays this way. These boys are thrilled to have been part of these elections. But like their countrymen, they are impatient for the more important national elections to take place. And that election will first require some notion of the political status of Kosovo. Should it remain a province of Serbia, and if so, with what degree of autonomy? Or, as Kosovo Albanians would have it, should Kosovo become an independent nation? The U.N. is nowhere near figuring this one out.

TUESDAY, OCTOBER 31, 2000

"I heard you say you used to teach art history, Teacher," Leonard told me last week, "so I think you might like an art show." He invited me to go with him to the art gallery run by UNMIK's Department of Culture where an American painter is being exhibited.

The gallery, a small, surprisingly tasteful building, sits in the middle of a large expanse of bare, hard-packed earth, dotted with clumps of weeds, broken bottles, and crushed Fanta cans. Downslope from the gallery is the Gaudi-gone-Cubist national library building, and to one side sits the massive, unfinished, heavily guarded Serbian Orthodox church, built, as Leonard tells me, in callous disregard of a promise to devote this land solely to university buildings.

Leonard and I are the only people in the gallery today, so we can walk around and talk freely about the paintings. It is excellent conversation practice for him. I am impressed with Leonard's eye, with his ability to look critically at color and composition, and with his appreciation for the way the artist has combined painting and photography. But it is the subject matter, portraits of young Albanian men and women painted right after the war, that makes quiet Leonard particularly eloquent, that causes him to ask me repeatedly for the right English words. "How do you say what her eyes tell us, Teacher, when you know she is remembering something terrible and will never be able to forget?"

"Haunted," I suggest, and tell him what the word means. "Yes," Leonard nods, staring at the picture in front of us. "Her eyes are haunted."

WEDNESDAY, NOVEMBER 1, 2000

Today Ed and I walk Qeni (Albanian for dog, and pronounced "*chay'-ney*"), the big, lovable office dog, up Dragodan. By the time we reach the top of the hill we've collected *thirteen* little boys! They are drawn by this odd American couple who have hitched a dog to a rope and are walking down the street with him! Pets are not the norm here. For most Kosovo Albanians, pets are a luxury. Most dogs and cats are feral, and big dogs such as Qeni are invariably fierce guard dogs. So these kids don't know what to make of our fondness for our playful malamute. They are both enchanted by him and terrified of him. Ed puts his hand up and into Qeni's mouth, demonstrating that he's gentle, friendly. One by one the little guys approach, giving Qeni a quick pat on the rump and darting off, giggling. After a while they can't keep their hands off him, and compete to see who gets to hold the rope. We are a noisy, happy procession along the dirt road at the crest of Dragodan.

THURSDAY, NOVEMBER 2, 2000

Sheryl is all energy. She gets up early every morning to jog, braving the polluted air and miles of mud or, alternately, dust. She has somehow managed to get into KFOR's gym, the only place to work out in the city, where she exercises with the soldiers. There is no task she won't tackle, no obstacle she won't challenge. She takes no guff from anybody. Before Kosovo, she was staff attorney for an organization in New York City that worked with disadvantaged young people and afterward practiced with a New York law firm. She is young, tough, cute, and lots of fun.

Today we meet for soggy "pizza" downtown and discuss for a few minutes the "Dogs of CEELI." She laughs and tells me Ed has become the "dog man" to the little kids in ABA-CEELI's neighborhood. Each day a group of little boys knocks on the door to ask Ed if he will let them pat Qeni, which, of course, he does. Sheryl has just rescued another dog, a puppy, which she's keeping in the office's downstairs bathroom until she can find someone to adopt it. And Kate, kind-hearted Kate, has rescued the most pitiful animal in the Balkans, an old, crippled, hairless, half-dead mutt who wandered in the gate and who is now being fed by Kate and Fexhi. Fexhi has built "Hey" (as in "Hey, you!") a shelter in the backyard, and to everyone's astonishment, Hey is still alive.

Our conversation turns to old and new boyfriends (hers), old boyfriends (mine), her career in law, my career in public relations and marketing, our reactions to life in Kosovo. She and Kate are sharing a nice apartment downtown and are learning to live with the noise and confusion, dust and pollution. We find a lot to laugh about and a lot to complain about. We are American women having lunch.

It strikes me that for the international community, Kosovo is like an ocean liner—people come together quickly and with an intensity born of isolation, loneliness, and a common purpose. Kate, Sheryl, Ed and I would never have met each other in the U.S.—we're from Florida, New York, and California, and live very different kinds of lives—but because we've been thrown together here in war-ravaged Prishtina, we immediately came to know, depend upon, and trust each other.

FRIDAY, NOVEMBER 3, 2000

Another young woman has joined the class. She came into the room after class had started and, in a voice so soft I could hardly hear her, said that she knew the class was full, but the manager had said she could ask if I would let her in anyway. I'm worried about the class size, but how could I say no to this sweet young woman with the face of a Ghirlandaio Madonna? I ask her to find a seat and have the class introduce themselves. "I am Drita," she says with exquisite shyness. I ask her to stay after class for a moment, and, when class is over, ask if she would like to come in thirty minutes or so before each class so I can help her get caught up. She has a heartbreaking smile, slow and tender and full of hope. "I would like that, Teacher, yes. I thank you very much."

SATURDAY, NOVEMBER 4, 2000

I hear it over and over. From Ahmet, the owner of the Cambridge School: "Americans saved our lives." Faton, my student who recently graduated from the university here in physics, told me "We love America, Teacher. We love Clinton. To us Madeleine Albright is like Mother Teresa. We love her. She brought the bombs that drove the Serbs out of Kosova." And again tonight from Fatmir, the owner of the bootleg video store where Agim has taken me to rent, for 40 cents, a copy of *The Patriot* (videotaped by someone sitting in a theater): "You Americans gave us our lives back. Americans care about us, you understand us."

As he speaks, I feel a wave of guilt. For one thing, I know that help from the U.S. and NATO came late, that we made many mistakes. But, with Britain's Tony Blair and our Madeleine Albright encouraging him, Clinton did authorize the "humanitarian intervention," the NATO bombing, that drove Serb forces from the country.

And my uneasiness at the Kosovars' gratitude is personal, too. I must ask myself honestly, how much did *I* really care about the war in Kosovo at the time? Like most Americans, I watched on TV the endless lines of refugees, the comfortless improvised camps in the mountains where old people and young families with babies slept under plastic sheeting and hid among the trees, the huge tented cities looking like the concentration camps they were that sprang up on the borders, where aid workers were overwhelmed by over 800,000 hungry, terrified, exhausted human beings. But how much of my *attention* did I give it? I didn't so much as call the Red Cross to make a donation. Yet, here I am, an American in Kosovo, being given credit by my very Americanness for having saved the lives of a whole people. "Ah, American!" say the taxi drivers, the shopkeepers. "You saved us. We love you, we love America!"

And, sadly, I am beginning to understand that the hope, the optimism I see in this country, is based largely on America's interest, America's continued involvement in Kosovo. The Albanians I've met do not trust Europe (with the exception of Britain's Tony Blair) to act in Kosovo's best interest, to stay the course. But they think America will always be there for them. I am very much afraid that our interest as a nation is fickle. After all, we are famous for our short attention span. We will desert Kosovo at some point; then their American heroes will become American traitors. Where will they find hope then? To whom will they look?

SUNDAY, NOVEMBER 5, 2000

Ed has persuaded me to drop in on a soccer game at the big stadium downtown. Only a handful of spectators, mostly fathers with their young sons. I am the only woman in the stands. The teams, Ed says, are pretty good. As we watch, a young boy, about eleven, with a wiry little body and a killer smile, passes in front of us holding a tray of pumpkin seeds. "He just winked at me!" I tell Ed, delighted. In a couple of minutes he returns and plops himself down by Ed. Again that smile aimed at each of us in turn. He gives each of us some pumpkin seeds—samples, we think, so he can sell us more later. We exchange names by etching them on the concrete floor with a pop-top tab. Bajram is his name. We shake hands. He observes that Ed is eating his seeds incorrectly. He shows Ed how to crack the husk and remove the tasty kernel inside. He inches even closer to Ed, almost protectively, until his body is flush up against Ed's. He takes each of our hands and pours out a Russian teaglass full of seeds into our palms. We decide we should pay him now for his seeds, his attention. A Deutschemark, maybe? But no! Bajram will have none of our money! Maybe because we are foreigners, maybe because we are a "mother and father" and with the addition of his "child," we are now a family, and family is everything here in Kosovo. At the very least we are now his friends, and he will not take money from his friends. We know all this though not a word has been spoken between us. As we leave the stadium he rushes after us to give us yet another handful of seeds, with yet another smile and a touch on the arm.

Ed is almost in tears as we leave. This is what we have seen everywhere here. A kindness, a warmth, a willingness to express affection through touch. As in many places in Europe, women walk arm in arm, men hug and kiss, friends interact with an easy proximity. But here—maybe because the *need* for it is so great—it seems to us there exists an extra measure of sweetness and trust. It is something we are overwhelmed by every day.

MONDAY, NOVEMBER 6, 2000

Driving around the countryside with Ed today, I am suddenly disoriented. Not as to *where* we are, but as to *when* we are. Looking at the ruined villages, then again at Prishtina, the small ragged city sitting in its bowl, I feel I'm living in the Middle Ages. For surely the horrors visited on Kosovo last year could not have occurred in *our* enlightened era. Surely they belong to a darker, less civilized period. Don't they?

TUESDAY, NOVEMBER 7, 2000

Another Granit has joined our class. A serious-looking young man with brown curly hair, and dark, penetrating eyes—quite the opposite of the first Granit to join the class, a true scamp with a quick grin and eyes full of mischief. "How will you know which Granit I call on?" I ask the two Granits, laughing.

"Call them Granit 1 and Granit 2, Teacher!" Luan suggests. The Granits are delighted and the class roars approval. So, Granit 1 and Granit 2 they are.

What are their stories, these two very different Granits? How did they survive the years of apartheid? How did they survive the war? I wonder this about everyone I meet.

Later...

Tonight lying in bed with my journal I wonder about young Serbs in Kosovo. About the gypsy children and young people of other minorities. There aren't many left. Most have fled, fearing Albanian reprisals. But there are some, living hunkered-down lives in a country that doesn't want them anymore. They need help, too. Who is teaching them?

Thursday, November 9, 2000

Last week I brought for Luan, my mechanical engineer-poet, my favorite poem, Mary Oliver's "Winter at Herring Cove." He has studied it and brings it back to me today, marked and noted. He reads slowly, awkwardly:

Years ago,
in the bottle-green light
of the cold January sea . . .

"What is it, Teacher, this 'bottle-green light'?" he asks, and nods thoughtfully as I explain.

In class I ask about their favorite writers. They almost all mention Ismail Kadare, whose book, *The Palace of Dreams,* was banned in his native Albania under the paranoid, brutal rule of Enver Hoxha. When these students speak of "their" writers or musicians or artists, they are speaking of any Albanian, whether from Kosovo or Albania or Macedonia or, for that matter, from anywhere in the Western diaspora. There is "Kosova," their country. And there is their ethnicity, "Albanian." Their identity is linked to both.

On my way home, I stop at the Dukagjini bookstore, the only store in town with books in English, and find a copy of Kadare's book.

Tonight at home Ed and I watch soccer on an Italian channel. Italy versus Croatia. The announcers scream the play-by-play in frenzied nonstop Italian that we can't begin to decipher. After a while, Ed turns to me, deadpan, and says, "For all I know they're debating the Albigensian Heresy."

I turn in early—having enjoyed all the soccer I can stand, as my father would say—and before writing my journal entry, begin to read *The Palace of Dreams.* It is, from the beginning, a nightmarish fable of the spirit-crushing effects of totalitarian power. Kadare has envisioned a state that seeks to monitor, control, and punish even the nightly dreams of its people. I can see why this book is dear to the hearts of Albanians, both in Albania and in Kosovo. And I can see why Hoxha banned it.

FRIDAY, NOVEMBER 10, 2000

Ah, the playful exhibitionism of the young people of Prishtina! Jehona, always striking, wears tall burgundy boots and a smart gray skirt to Ed's office today. Edona, a fifteen-year-old beauty in my class, wears a fashionable pink cowl sweater, her hair and makeup the envy of any Western model. And on the streets the young people are strutting their stuff—teenaged girls sport fashionable square-toed high-heeled boots, the young men black leather jackets and counterfeit designer jeans. Surely this is a healthy sign, an indication that in spite of the recent horrors of their lives, there is still life and spirit and self-confidence here.

SATURDAY, NOVEMBER 11, 2000

Today I meet my students in front of the school and walk them up the hill to our house for our first meeting of the Hemingway Book Club of Kosova. Almost everyone has shown up, most, I expect, as much out of curiosity about Teacher's house and husband as out of interest in the book. Still, whatever it takes.

Faton, Amira, Edona, the two Granits, Luan, Leutrim, Leonard, Besart, Niti, Genti, Fazile, Silvete, Dafina. My sweet Drita, who lives in a village outside of town, cannot get a ride in on Saturday.

I seat them in the downstairs parlor where we have cookies and juice. They meet Ed, standing up politely as he enters the room, offering their hands and a smile. When Ed leaves, they ask me about him. "What does your husband do in California, Teacher? Why does he want to work in Kosova?"

"Ed teaches at McGeorge Law School in Sacramento now," I tell them. "It's part of the University of the Pacific. But early in his career he was a civil rights and legal services lawyer. That means he worked to protect the rights of minorities and poor people in our country. He wanted to come to Kosovo to help build a legal system that will protect the human rights of everyone in your country."

They seem immensely pleased with this, satisfied that they have placed Ed in the general scheme of things. But I doubt it has occurred to them that Ed will be working to protect the rights not only of Albanians, but of Serbs, Roma, and other groups who are the actual minorities in Kosovo now.

They now eagerly devour the photos of our house on the cliff over the ocean, of the coastline, our family. "Is this what houses in California are like, Teacher?" "You can see the ocean from your parlor, Teacher!" "Your sons are so handsome, Teacher!" They admire the photograph of my father proudly displaying his big trout, of my mother in her southern garden. I tell them I grew up in a very small town in the southern part of the U.S. where my parents still live. Then they ask me about my sons. They won't know me until they know my family, it is clear. I tell them our oldest son, Brian, my stepson, is studying to be a paleoanthropologist—and explain what that means. "*Old,* old humans!" He is married to Amy. "And they have children, Teacher?" They seem disappointed when I tell them, "Not yet."

They beg me to continue. My stepson Paul lives in Spain and is teaching English and studying flamenco culture. He is an accomplished flamenco guitarist. And my son Paul ("two Pauls, Teacher!") is a police detective in California. Granit 1 and Besart are interested in this news. They, too, would like to become policemen, they tell me, "because here there are many criminals who would ruin our country," as Besart says.

They are fascinated by the American magazines we've brought with us, and even more, they are thrilled to see we have books about Kosovo. It surprises and delights them to find there is enough interest in their country for people in other parts of the world to write and to read books about it. All this is a revelation for these students, most of whom have been isolated from the rest of the world their whole lives.

We go upstairs to what Ed and I have come to call the "Red Salon" where the long sofas easily accommodate everyone. Then we get out our Hemingway and read the opening paragraph:

> He was an old man who fished alone in a skiff in the Gulf Stream and he had gone eighty-four days now without taking a fish. In the first forty days a boy had been with him. But after forty days without a fish the boy's parents had told him that the old man was now definitely and finally *salao,* which is the worst form of unlucky, and the boy had gone at their orders in another boat which caught three good fish the first week. It made the boy sad to see the old man come in each day with his skiff empty and he always went down to help him carry either the coiled lines or the gaff and harpoon and the sail that was furled around the mast. The sail was patched with flour sacks and, furled, it looked like the flag of permanent defeat.

It's hard to say if the spare elegance of Hemingway's language, the rhythm and power of any of these lines, will translate well to these Albanian speakers. But we can concentrate on the story—I know they will understand the story.

"What does Hemingway tell us in these first few pages about the old man?"

"He cannot catch any fish," Leutrim says.

"He is very poor," Luan adds.

"He is old and so maybe is not so strong as he was," says Faton.

"That sounds pretty bad," I comment. "Is there anything else?"

"He has a boat."

There is silence as they realize that the old man possesses nothing but his boat and his shack.

"So," I say, "does the old man really have almost nothing?"

"Teacher," says Genti, "he has the little boy, Manolin, who loves him."

"Yes," I tell them. "Manolin loves the old man as his guide, his teacher, his great friend. He has absolute faith in the old man." I read from the book:

"And the best fisherman is you."

"No. I know others better."

"*Que va,*" the boy said. "There are many good fisherman and some great ones. But there is only you."

"Thank you. You make me happy. I hope no fish will come along so great that he will prove us wrong."

"There is no such fish if you are still strong as you say."

"I may not be as strong as I think," the old man said, "but I know many tricks and I have resolution."

"Yes," says Granit 2, really interested now, "and the old man has, I think, great courage. Even though he has not caught a fish, he has not stopped. He keeps trying." Granit 2's manner is serious, somber, even. He seems prematurely burdened with extra years. But he is one of the brightest kids in the class; his dark eyes are alive with curiosity. I can tell that he relishes the chance to read this book.

"So, in spite of his bad luck, he has hope that things will be better," I offer. "He has a spirit that will not give up." I read aloud another line:

Everything about him was old except his eyes and they were the same color as the sea and were cheerful and undefeated.

"I wonder," I ask, "if you know anyone who has been through very hard times and is still 'cheerful and undefeated'?"

Most everyone identifies family members—parents, grandparents, a sister, an uncle—who have suffered but have continued to struggle, and have somehow maintained their optimism, their joy of living.

"And how about you?" I ask them.

I see light coming into their eyes as they begin to understand that the old man's struggle, his endurance, describe their own lives, the recent history of their country. Will they come to see that they are the heroes of their own stories? These young people know about "undefeated." They live it every day.

SUNDAY, NOVEMBER 12, 2000

At 2 p.m. Igballe bangs on the front door, motioning me to come quickly outside. There is a wedding reception going on across the street. Lovely attendants with carefully coiffed hair and traditional Albanian white dresses, vests spangled with gold thread and sequins, beating tambourines and singing. The white-veiled bride coming down the steps of her house clinging to the arms of her father and brother. As she gets into the car with her new husband, the driver pulls a pistol from his dark suit and shoots several rounds into the air. Other young men take out their guns and join him. Igballe, her neighbors, and I—all of us middle-aged women who have been watching the bride teary-eyed—frown at each other, wincing at the sharp sounds. Men and their guns.

Later this evening I have dinner with Isa, Igballe, and Agim, who will translate for us. A delicious traditional pita, a pie three feet in diameter and baked in an oven outside, its delicate pastry filled with spinach and goat cheese, served with a bowl of yogurt and sliced apples. Why was the bride weeping? I ask them. "Because she is leaving her parents," Igballe tells me. "Children here do not want to leave their parents."

"She cries because she is getting married!" Agim laughs. "She will never be free again!"

I ask about divorce. They seem a bit shocked to learn that both Ed and I have been married before. Divorce is practically nonexistent here, they say. "If my father were to leave my mother," Agim explains, "her brothers would come find him and beat him up, shoot him maybe." I gather that he is only half-joking.

Isa shrugs and grins as if to say, "We are still a bit backward here."

MONDAY, NOVEMBER 13, 2000

I think again as I putter around this morning how lucky we are to have found this house, how much more comfortable we are than I had imagined we would be. It's hard to remember now why the house seemed so strange, so alien when we first saw it. I look around and try to recapture that strangeness. Of course, most things don't really work. Drawers don't close, doors don't open, the stove heats erratically, the washing machine turns clothes a grim gray, the color of putty, then chews them up and floods the bathroom floor. The radiators don't heat, the tiny freezer compartment in the tiny refrigerator doesn't freeze, the water and electricity are likely to disappear at any moment and there is no phone system.

And then there is that neo-Ottoman décor that so stunned us when we first saw it. The plush red velvet and wooly sheepskins and shiny lacquered furniture. The thick velour bedspread with the face of a large growling tiger that Igballe was so proud to offer us. (Tiger, tiger, burning bright, in this strange Prishtina night.) The carefully arranged plastic flowers and the ornamental birds made of seashells.

When we moved in, I replaced these ornaments with our family photos and magazines from home, hoping Igballe would not be offended if I moved her things to lower shelves. When she comes each week to clean she dusts her glass and plastic *objets* with a tenderness that tells me she misses her home, her things. Yet, she has never shown even the slightest resentment or bitterness. She and Isa remain hospitable, cheerful, eager to make our stay here a pleasant one. Like most Kosovars we've met, they are wonderful, warm people, and I've come to love them, to enjoy their company even though, still, we cannot say a word to each other.

And indeed, they are in the house often, fixing one thing or another. The wiring in the house is problematic, to say the least. So far three space heaters in this parlor have self-destructed as I sat nearby. Fire flying from the outlet, plugs melting, the burned wires dropping off the plugs. Isa says he's fixed it now, but I expect he's simply put a fresh plastic cover over the outlet so we can't see what's going on behind it. And to give him credit, this does constitute "fixing" here. Out of sight, out of mind. Wait for the next catastrophe and hope for the best.

Funny how quickly—and happily—one can adopt that philosophy.

TUESDAY, NOVEMBER 14, 2000

Several hundred people from Gjakova have come to Prishtina to protest the ongoing imprisonment by the Serbs of their young men. Today I walk downtown to photograph them. Old, old men and women whose sons and grandsons are missing or have been in prison in Serbia since 1998 and 1999. The Serbs say they're terrorists. Albanians call them political prisoners. Wives, sisters, sons, and daughters, all holding large photos of their loved ones, camping out in the cold November nights in the middle of Mother Teresa Boulevard. They have been here for three days and nights now, hoping to attract media attention and, with it, the support of the world. But so far there has been only local coverage. Today I am the only photographer in sight. No one outside Prishtina hears their protest, sees their photos or their sad, weary faces. Speakers come to the microphone. A young woman, just released from prison, tells of her son being born in her cell, of the jeering prison guards who named the baby "Slobodan." "Ko*so-o*-va!" she wails. "Ko*so-o*-va!"

Soon, I know, these families will return to their homes, defeated, despairing.

WEDNESDAY, NOVEMBER 15, 2000

Tonight, after class and our tutorial, Leonard and I walk out onto the streets, dark now even at 6, to look for a taxi. There are no taxis, few cars. Except for groups of young men in their black leather jackets walking down the middle of the streets, the city is deserted. Ah, it is the demonstration, I remember. The city has shut down. We walk up Mother Teresa and over to a side street where, Leonard says, there's a taxi stand. And so there is, but there are no taxis. Leonard knocks on the window of a small car just pulling out from the curb. The man, Leonard says, translating, is not a taxi driver, but can drive me to Dragodan after he picks up his daughter.

In a reckless moment I say "O.K." and climb in. After all, the man is picking up his daughter so he must be a good guy, right? Leonard looks worried. My gut does a little turn, telling me I should be worried, too. But the driver has pulled out onto the street now and I am committed. I wave goodbye to Leonard and look over at my companion. Streetlights show me a large middle-aged man with a roundish, attractive face wearing a rumpled suit and open-necked shirt. The car is old and small and, like most cars here, rather shabby. I venture an introduction and say, "My name is Paula, and I'm from America." He grins widely and his right hand comes off the wheel to take mine—a huge paw pumping my bony fingers. "Ismet!" he says, loudly. "My name Ismet! America! Americans saved us! I love Americans! God and Americans! Americans and God!"

Ismet doesn't talk, he shouts. His voice, his presence fill the car. He gesticulates wildly as he talks, somehow keeping one hand on the steering wheel most of the time. He philosophizes at the top of his voice. "All mens the same! All mens can be good! I believe we can have peace! But Serbs, no! First they must say they sorry for what they did!" It is the first time I've heard an Albanian even imply that there might be hope for understanding with the Serbs. But Ismet doesn't elaborate. He goes back to his favorite theme, America. "My daughter, my Number Three daughter"—he has five daughters, he says—"she go to America in January, live with American family, study hard! We love America!"

He runs a red light and swings up over a median, then lurches onto a vacant lot, hard-packed, deep-rutted dirt, bump, bump, bumping along until we slide off onto another street. Then, suddenly, we're in a tunnel. Dark, with deep, even darker recesses off to the sides. There is little traffic. I didn't know there was a tunnel in Prishtina and once again a tiny trembling at the edge of my gut tells me I should be afraid. I should be asking myself what I am doing here in a dark tunnel with a total stranger in a wartorn city in the middle of the Balkans. Instead, I am relishing Ismet's enthusiasm and wondering, as if I'm reading a story about someone else, what will happen next. Just as I think this tunnel has no end, Ismet swerves and suddenly we are outside again, on another squalid street where, standing under a streetlamp like an angel in the midst of an inferno, I see a delicate blond-headed little girl in a pink sweater, wearing glasses, who can only be the object of our quest. He pulls up next to her and as she climbs into the back seat he says proudly, "Tringa! My daughter!"

Tringa is charming. She shakes my hand quite seriously, and as her father has boasted her English is very good even though she is only seven years old. At her father's request, she writes her name, his name, and their phone number on a slip of paper and solemnly hands it to me. She is as reserved as her father is gregarious. It is clear they adore each other.

"I trade my five daughters for your three sons!" Ismet jokes. But I can tell he wouldn't trade his daughters for all the sons in Kosovo.

Another five minutes and we arrive at Ed's office on Dragodan. Ismet says he would like my husband and me to visit his home, to take a meal with them. I tell him truthfully that I would like that very much, and I thank him for the ride. "Ah!" he booms, beaming. "You are American, I take you to Istanbul if you want to go!" He reaches out to shake my hand, and I grasp his with both of mine. He puts his left hand over mine and, reaching from the back seat, Tringa puts her tiny hand on top of ours. There is a lump in my throat, and for a moment the car is silent.

Somehow, in Kosovo, each such encounter fills my soul; every parting breaks my heart.

THURSDAY, NOVEMBER 16, 2000

The Hemingway Book Club of Kosova has changed everything. Before I started the club, we were just a class. A good class, a friendly class, even a fun class. But now something remarkable has happened. We are a club, a group of people who share a special link with each other. Even those whose English is not strong enough to follow the book easily know that the book club has connected us in a new, more intimate way.

Since our first club meeting last Saturday, more students are taking me up on my offer of special tutoring and are staying for conversation practice after class. Many are asking me for advice on career choices. And, of course, they are asking for more American literature. The class now *is* the club, and we're beginning to feel like a family.

Luan comes up to me after class and hands me a small packet. "This is for you, Teacher. I think you like to have it, maybe." Inside are photographs of his family and fellow villagers in the mountain forest where they all spent three months in 1998 after Serb security forces burned their village. They were part of some 250,000 Albanians who were displaced that year as Serb police and other security forces terrorized small towns and villages, prompting the KLA to strike back. And so it went all year, an endless cycle of escalating violence in which Kosovar civilians such as Luan were trapped.

There they are in his photos—Luan's elderly grandfather in his white felt *plis,* his mother in her headscarf and *dimija,* the baggy pajama-like trousers favored by rural women, his sister-in-law and baby nephew all sitting on the ground in the forest. And there is their tent pieced together from plastic sheeting, looking like a puff of wind would tear it apart and blow it away.

I ask if they lived in terror during that time in the mountains. He shrugs. The KLA, he says, were between the Serb paramilitaries and Luan's mountain refuge, so the villagers felt relatively safe. "It was the first time we saw armed people who were there to protect us, not kill us," he says.

It's easy to see why the KLA are heroes to many Albanians here. Tim Judah, whose book on Kosovo has helped Ed and me understand so much of what has happened here, calls the KLA "the most successful guerilla movement in modern history." Many Serbs, Roma, and other minority groups in Kosovo, and some internationals, consider the KLA to be nothing more than thugs and drug traffickers who didn't hesitate to kill their Albanian countrymen if they were suspected of collaboration with the Serbs. But Luan, like most Albanians, sees them simply as the saviors of his family.

FRIDAY, NOVEMBER 17, 2000

After school Leonard and I walk to his apartment building. His parents have invited me for a visit. Leonard is nervous and says, "Teacher, you must remember that some people do not have grand houses, some people have only a small place to live." Leonard has been to our house on Dragodan, and it pains me that he is apologizing for what I am about to see.

His building is a drab cinder-block low-rise just off Mother Teresa. We walk up the dank concrete stairwell, its walls spray-painted with graffiti. Leonard's parents and his sister are at their front door, waiting for me. I shake hands with Zerife, his mother, Mehdi, his father, and his little sister, Nora. As I stoop to unlace my shoes, Zerife is ahead of me, insisting that she do it for me.

They usher me into their tiny parlor. It is about ten feet long, and five feet wide at the end where the sofa sits, widening to about seven feet near the door. The sofa and two chairs, lined up against one wall, are covered in old, tattered sheepskins. The walls are dingy, the only bright spot a cluster of pink plastic flowers on the TV. They ask me to sit at the near end of the sofa. Leonard and Nora sit on one side of me, their parents in chairs on the other side. Zerife leaves, to return with glasses of juice and small plates of sliced bananas and apples, slices of cake. She pulls up her chair as close to me as she can get, and starts to talk.

"My mother says to tell you, 'Thank you for coming to our home. And thank you for coming to our country to help us. And thank you for helping our son, Leonard, who is a good boy, a gentle boy.'" Leonard blushes as he translates this part.

Zerife is in her late thirties. She is short and buxom and in her face I can see the pretty young girl she once was. She wears a threadbare, faded sweater and laughs easily and often.

Mehdi is still a handsome man. He wears a thin blue cotton sports coat, a striped open-necked shirt. He is quiet, shy, like his son. But he has an air of melancholy, of profound weariness, that his son doesn't share. Leonard has told me that his father worries every day that his teacher's pay of $130 a month won't continue to feed the family.

Both Mehdi and Zerife look ten years older than they are. They appear unhealthy, their skin has a grayish pallor. Each of them is missing some teeth. It is as if they have spent years channeling all the available health to their children.

"My mother says, 'We cannot believe we would ever have sitting in our home an American, and so kind an American who help us so much.'" I am embarrassed, and say to Zerife, "It is a great privilege for me to teach your son. He is a very bright, kind-hearted young man. My sons are far away in the United States. I thank you for sharing your son with me while I am in Kosovo."

I eat. They have eaten earlier, they say, but I wonder if they're giving me all their food. We chat. Every now and then Zerife thanks me again for coming to see them, for coming from America, for helping Leonard. They notice I have brought my camera with me and ask me to take pictures. We pose, Zerife and me, arms around each other. Nora and me. Leonard and me. Leonard and his family. All possible configurations. I promise to bring them copies of the pictures.

As I return to the sofa in the narrow space between the coffee table and the wall, my sweater catches on a splinter. "This is our NATO splinter," Leonard tells me. And I see now that this cramped parlor must also be Leonard and his sister's bedroom, the place they were sleeping the night the NATO bomb blew out the window above them. After that night, they all moved into the even smaller kitchen, Leonard says, spending the rest of the war sleeping on the kitchen floor. I begin to realize the true horror of their three-month-long imprisonment in this cramped flat.

Zerife tells me more of their ordeal, her face somber now as she remembers. "One night two Serb policemen came. They tell us they will take Leonard away. And I know that means they will kill him." I reach out and put my hand on Zerife's arm, squeezing it gently as she talks. "So I give the big bad policeman some money. And the other, the younger one, I think, maybe he is an only son, too, and I ask him please not to take our only son away from us." Her eyes seem to search my face as if to say, You are a mother, too, so you must understand what this was like, to think that I would lose my son. I cannot begin to comprehend her terror, of course; I can only listen and hold on to her arm. "They search the house, looking for more money, even breaking the loaf of bread to see if we hide anything. Then they go away, we don't know why." Leonard thinks it was because the younger policeman felt sorry for his mother. His mother is not so sure.

Other policemen came to threaten and terrorize. But each time they were willing to take money rather than Leonard or Mehdi. "Every day we feared for the knock on the door. But we were a lucky family, I think." Zerife sighs and gets up to get more food.

Meanwhile, Mehdi has been waiting with questions, and he now asks me, quietly, what the houses are like in America. What weather is like in California. Are the universities large? Do the libraries have many books? "My father would like to see sometime a library with many books," Leonard explains. I answer the best I can.

"I understand you teach geography," I tell Mehdi. "I used to teach geography, too. The western hemisphere, to eighth graders."

Mehdi brightens. "Amazon!" he says.

"Orinoco!" I counter.

"Mississippi!"

"Colorado!"

"Rio de la Plata!"

"Rio Grande!"

And so we have our geographical dialogue, our shared language the rivers of the western hemisphere. We have found a connection, and we smile at each other.

Mehdi leaves the room and returns shortly with a crumpled Xerox copy of a map of Kosova, and an old tourist-type brochure with a map and photos. I express interest in the maps and, too late, realize that to admire is to acquire. Medhi insists I take them. He would like me to have them so I will always remember Kosova. I silently resolve to bring him good, colorful maps of the world when I return from the U.S. in January.

Zerife returns with slices of delicious pita and Turkish coffee. With great sincerity I compliment the chef and Zerife sits next to me, putting her arm through mine. "My mother cannot explain to you how much your visit means to us," says Leonard.

Nora has been happily taking everything in, answering my questions about her school, her interest in dancing. Her mother suggests she show me one of the traditional Albanian dances she has been learning. So, listening to the music in her head, Nora dances with her two bright scarves, gracefully dipping and waving and twirling in the narrow space by the door. I take photo after photo, and clap my hands, delighted.

As Nora sits again, her mother suggests suddenly, "Would you like to see Nora's hair?" Leonard explains, "My sister has beautiful hair. It has not been cut since she was three."

Of course I would. Nora smiles shyly as she unclasps the large plastic barrette at the back of her head. Her hair falls, *cascades* around her and I see that it is true. She has the most beautiful hair I have ever seen. Soft light brown waves edged with gold. I let out an involuntary sigh of pure pleasure at the sight. Leonard, Mehdi, and Zerife beam. "Ah!" Zerife has another idea. "Maybe you would like to see Nora dance with her hair down?"

Nora has begun to be embarrassed now, but when I say I would like that, she dances again, and this time she flings her head so that her hair flies about her, making the dance both wilder and more graceful.

I am sorry when I see it is time for me to go. I thank them again for their hospitality, for the food, for the dance. "My mother and father say," says Leonard, "they have never had such a happy day. The war brought a kind American to our home, a new friend. The war has done a good thing."

Suddenly I am overcome by their kindness, their gratitude, by the special place they have given me in their lives. And when Zerife insists again on lacing my shoes up, I begin to protest. But Leonard tells me once again, "Please, my mother wants to do this for you." On the stairwell Zerife supports my arm with one hand, then stoops, and with the other hand holds a cigarette lighter at my feet to light my way down the dark steps. I stumble anyway, but it is my tears, not the darkness, that blind me. Please, Zerife, I think, don't. Don't treat me like a queen, a celebrity. I don't deserve this. I don't deserve your gratitude, your devotion. Leonard probably won't be admitted to an American school. I can do nothing for your poverty. I cannot restore your health. It is *you,* Zerife, you and your family, who should be treated as royalty. It is *you* who are extraordinary, who deserve thanks and praise and devotion.

I suddenly feel I am a fraud, an imposter, in this country. It is all I can do to keep from sobbing as Zerife pulls me close to her, putting her arm through mine to walk me to the taxi stand.

I am stunned by the love in this sweet family, by their willingness to share that love with me, and as I ride in the taxi toward my home on "rich man's hill," I think of Zerife and Mehdi who count their treasures in their son's gentle nature and their daughter's beautiful hair.

I came to this country to pay tribute to the people here, to their courage and endurance. And everywhere I turn they, with their grateful and generous hearts, keep turning the tables. I feel shaken, disoriented, unworthy, inadequate to any expectation. I am here under false pretenses. Tonight, trying to explain all this to Ed, I can't stop crying.

Later . . .

Lying in bed around midnight I read from Agate Nesaule who, in *A Woman in Amber* describes her ordeal as a displaced person in World War II Germany. She says, "We have to believe that even the briefest human connections can heal. Otherwise, life is unbearable." Tonight, I hope with all my heart that she is right, that just making the human connection can make a difference. It is, really, all I have to offer.

SUNDAY, NOVEMBER 19, 2000

A day to sleep late and, while having leisurely coffee in bed, our conversation turns to the four Ashkali (Albanian-speaking Roma—

the most assimilated Gypsies in Kosovo), who, having been escorted this week for their protection by UNHCR (United Nations High Commissioner for Refugees) from Serbia back to their former homes in Kosovo, were left in their village and were found dead the next day. Three men and a boy. Shot, execution style. The Albanian villagers, their neighbors, say they didn't hear a thing.

I asked my students about the Roma, who most believe were collaborators with the Serbs. Leonard says his uncle, who lives in a village in the south, saw Roma help Serb paramilitaries kill twenty of his neighbors. Leonard's little cousins, girls seven and eight, also witnessed the murders. They still have nightmares about it. And during the war, Leonard, from his hidden perch at his window above the street, often saw Roma walking with Serb police.

Although most Albanians seem to regard them as mere opportunists rather than racist ideologues like the Serbs, there is no love here for the Roma. Tens of thousands of Roma are now in wretched refugee camps in border countries, and if they return they might find their houses burned by furious Albanians, or, like these Ashkali, they might well be murdered. Once again, the many suffering for the crimes of the few.

I wonder: A year ago today, at home on the ocean, what would Ed's and my weekend morning-in-bed conversation have been about?

MONDAY, NOVEMBER 20, 2000

"We were here first," the students tell me today. We are discussing after class the history of Kosovo and they are determined to prove to me that this is their, the Albanians', rightful homeland. Leonard explains, "The Illyrians, Teacher. You know them. They are our ancestors. They were here thousands of years ago. Before anybody else. You can read it in books. It is true."

Yes. But there has been a lot of mixing and moving around through the centuries, and the truth is that no one really knows exactly who was where, when, and in what numbers. As Noel Malcolm says in *Kosovo: A Short History,* the conflict here is as much about conflicting views of history and national origins as it is about anything else. In any case, he says, "It can never be said too often that questions of chronological priority in ancient history—who got there first—are simply irrelevant to deciding the rights and wrongs of any present-day political situation."

Like Jews and Palestinians in Israel/Palestine, both Serbs and Albanians have historical claims to Kosovo. The issue is not who has the strongest or oldest claim, but how everyone can live together peacefully *now.*

I don't argue with the students, though, or say anything about Kosovo, the Illyrians, the Albanians, or the Serbs. But I do mention Native Americans and European immigrants in the U.S. There are some puzzled faces as they think about that one.

TUESDAY, NOVEMBER 21, 2000

This morning, reading an e-mail from my brother David, I learn that a dear childhood companion has died. His memorial service has already been held. Completely unexpected, an aneurism that took him quickly as he slept. Tonight, I feel lonely. I am so far away from my friends and family, both in California and in my small hometown in Arkansas. I want to mourn with those who knew Jim and loved him. No one here in Prishtina knew Jim, could understand.

I call the school to say I'm sick. About 3:40, Leonard calls. Miraculously he has found a phone that works, and through another miracle my cell phone is working as well. His voice is worried. "You are sick, Teacher?"

I tell him I am sick at heart, that my friend died.

"I am so sorry, Teacher," his sweet voice comes to me as I lie listless on the sofa. "I know your heart is not in Kosova now. It is in your home with your friends. Life is sometimes very hard. This I have learned. But we must keep going. That is all. We must keep going."

Tonight I need the comforting embrace of that small southern town I grew up in. For the first time, I feel one of the pains—surely one of the greatest—of the expatriate. But the words of this eighteen-year-old Kosovar boy have come to me over the crackling phone line and have given me more comfort than I thought was possible.

Wednesday, November 22, 2000

Before class several students ask for help with some of the words in *The Old Man and the Sea*: "porpoise," "iridescent," "plankton," "prisms." They are really getting excited about the book, but it occurs to me that I'm not sure just what they know about Hemingway himself. So when everyone arrives, I ask:

"Who *was* Ernest Hemingway, anyway?"

"He was a very good writer, famous everywhere, even in Kosova," Granit 1 says.

Leutrim is eager to add what he knows. "He was a big man and had hair on his face"—"A beard," I offer— "and he liked adventures. He went to some wars and shot animals in Africa."

So they, like the rest of the world, have been caught up in the mystique of Hemingway the famous writer, the adventurer, the man of action. But they don't know any specifics.

"During the First World War," I tell them, "when he was only eighteen, he volunteered to drive an ambulance for the Red Cross in Italy so he could get into action. He was severely wounded in battle and spent a long time recovering."

This piques the boys' interest.

"Then in 1936 he went to Spain to report on the bloody civil war going on there. He wanted Americans to know that the Fascists under Franco and supported by Nazi Germany were waging a new kind of war in which there was no such thing as a noncombatant."

These students know about "total war," about the suffering of noncombatants. Suddenly, Hemingway has become very real to them.

We go on to discuss Hemingway's exploits as a journalist in World War II, when he was present both at D-Day and the liberation of Paris.

"You know," I say, finally, "if Hemingway had been alive in 1998 and 1999, I'm quite sure he would have come to Kosovo." They beam at this idea. "Do you know why?"

There is silence for a while as they think about it.

"Because he would have admired our struggle," Faton suggests.

"Because he liked fighting, and here was fighting."

"Yes, for both of those reasons," I tell them. "Hemingway knew that war was a terrible thing. But he knew that sometimes you have to fight. I think he would have agreed that in Kosova it was necessary to fight.

"And I think he would have admired your spirit, too," I continue. "He would have respected the way you never gave up hope, even when things seemed hopeless."

We go on to discuss our grammar lesson for the day, but I think we are all happily aware that we've added Ernest Hemingway to our group.

THURSDAY, NOVEMBER 23, 2000, THANKSGIVING

Kate and Sheryl have decided to have a real Thanksgiving dinner. So several of us temporary expats gather at their apartment tonight, each having scrounged the city to find ingredients for a "traditional" American dish. I found canned green beans earlier in the week, and added dried dill I brought from the U.S. I've also made candied carrots. Emily and Emmanuel (she a beautiful blond New Zealander, he a gregarious Haitian) have made a pumpkin pie, and Sheryl and Kate went to Macedonia and found a turkey—a Maryland-raised turkey! Henry has brought booze. The table is beautifully laid, and somehow it all really does feel like an American Thanksgiving. A couple of folks play guitar and we sing American folk songs, Beatles' tunes. As Kate, who has one of the loveliest voices I ever heard, plays guitar and sings "In My Life," tears roll down my face and I weep silently for Jim. No one seems to mind.

FRIDAY, NOVEMBER 24, 2000

After class some of us stay to talk about metaphor and symbol in *The Old Man and the Sea*. Hemingway said he didn't put any symbols in the book—"the sea is the sea, the fish is the fish"—but all of us bring to books our own lives, and we inevitably search for symbols to help us explain our experience. What will the students search for?

"The sea itself is perhaps the most powerful image in the book," I suggest. "What is the sea, do you think?"

There is much discussion until they finally agree that the sea is everything, it is our world, it is life. "It has good animals, like the flying fish, and bad animals, like the Portuguese man-of-war," says Amira. "The sea gives the old man happiness and it gives him sorrow and he must do the best he can with all of it."

"And how about the big fish the old man wants to catch," I ask. "What is Hemingway talking about here?"

"Ah, that is an easy one," Faton says. "The fish is the goal we all try to reach. Everyone wants one big fish. It is what we work and work for, but it is not simple. And sometimes it might be impossible."

We talk about our own "big fish," what each of us would like to do with our lives. Drita dreams of becoming an English teacher. Leutrim, surprisingly, wants to become a "doctor that helps womans"—a gynecologist. A few students giggle at this news, but Leutrim holds firm. A friend of his father's is a gynecologist, he says, and he admires the work he does for women. Leonard would like to do something with computers—he's not yet sure what. Faton's big fish is a Ph.D. in physics and an interesting, useful career. His struggle—like the struggle of all these students to reach their goals—is likely to be every bit as difficult as the old man's.

SATURDAY, NOVEMBER 25, 2000

It will be a long weekend. Kosovo's National Day is Monday, celebrating Albania's independence from the Turks in 1912. Because the Serbs refused permission to celebrate any sort of "Albanianness," this will be an especially festive day for Kosovo Albanians.

I am happy that they can celebrate, but as always, I am uneasy about any kind of nationalism. It is, by its nature, exclusive. It creates the "other," those who, because they are not of that nationality are, at the least, different. And from "different" it is so easy to go to "inferior," "unworthy," even "evil." We have seen what Serbian nationalism has done in the Balkans. And not just here, but all over the world, pride in *our* country, pride in *our* history, pride in *our* tribe or ethnic group or culture, has degenerated into contempt, suspicion, fear, then hatred of others. And the result—well, I see it here, all around me. I see it in the bombed buildings, the devastated countryside, the impoverished families.

Ed and I decide to explore an old section of the city where a large open market has brought into town many country folk. Usually Prishtina's streets are filled with young people, a study in youthful black. Black hair, black leather jackets, black pants and boots. But today I see old faces. Weathered, withered faces. Thin old men in their conical white *plis,* old women wearing headscarves, long coats and *dimija.* Here to sell their cabbages and leeks and onions and potatoes and peppers. Other vendors, the "Five and Dime" folks, spread blankets on the mud or put up rickety tables displaying their motley assortment of combs, batteries, bras, shoe polish, plastic bowls, knives, socks.

This is one of those rare occasions Ed and I get to see people from outside the city. Life in the country, in the small villages, is a world apart from life in Prishtina. Rural Kosovo was, we have heard, even before the war, more primitive than any place in Europe. Seeing these ragged country people here today reminds me that most of the students I'm teaching are not poor by Kosovo standards. My students are all middle-class urban Kosovars who may have had, before the war, a relatively comfortable life, and who even now can somehow scrape together twenty-five dollars each month to attend the Cambridge School.

No, the poorest, the least educated, those hit hardest by the war are in the countryside and in the isolated mountain villages. And how the city folk look down on these country folk! To hear some of our local city friends talk about them—"ignorant, filthy, stupid"— you would think there's an Indian-style caste system here.

Proof again that we humans will always find reasons to despise each other.

MONDAY, NOVEMBER 27, 2000

The concept of individual and family honor is at the core of the Kanun of Lek, and honor, the Kanun states, can often be upheld only with blood. Thus, the blood feud, which can last generations. Despite efforts to wipe out the blood feud—the folklorist Anton Çeta led the government in trying to call a general amnesty a few years ago—rural Albanians still kill each other over often trivial slights to someone's honor, slights that might have occurred decades earlier. The death of one person must be avenged with the death of another.

Tonight Ed and I discuss today's distressing UNMIK police report of a rural family in a car opening fire with automatic weapons on another family whose car then crashed into the car of a third family. The result of a long-standing feud. Many dead, many injured. In earlier times, Ed points out, revenge might have been by knife or some old rifle, keeping deaths to a minimum. But modern technology—grenades, automatic weapons, even automobiles—now offers the aggrieved a means of vengeance they haven't the discipline to use in moderation. They can now achieve in an instant a degree of carnage, he says, that in other times might have taken generations to accomplish.

TUESDAY, NOVEMBER 28, 2000

Today I teach modal verbs. I had never heard of modals until the ESL course I took before we left California. I sometimes feel I'm staying only one step ahead of my students. Knowing this could be boring, I'd devised a game, and had the class divide into teams, competing to see who knows the most uses of modals. I *must* go to school. *Would* you wake up? He *might* come with us. My God! I thought the walls would collapse and the school staff would come running in to tell us to quiet down! It's clear that games are going to be a good way for these *very competitive* students to learn. If we can just keep from alarming the rest of the school with our noise!

Downtown tonight to the Kosova Philharmonic concert. Wonderful! For a moment I feel like I am actually in Europe. A program of Mozart, Mendelssohn, Elgar, and a local composer, Valton Beqiri, whose music is very exciting. The audience huddles in folding chairs in coats and gloves and warm mufflers. It is so cold in the auditorium I can hardly move my fingers, so I don't see how the musicians manage. But they do. The first violinist has been imported from Albania, but all other musicians, including the conductor, are local. Ed and I wonder together: What happened to the orchestra's musical instruments during the war? Did this violinist smuggle his violin to the camp? Was this bassist's bass violin stolen or burned, and is this one a replacement? What have these musicians had to endure to be able to come together again for this victorious concert?

After the last note is sounded, a little girl rushes from the audience to the bassist, obviously her daddy, who gives her a big hug. She sits quietly on the platform beside him as the orchestra plays an encore. Our delighted applause lasts a long, long time.

WEDNESDAY, NOVEMBER 29, 2000

I've struggled with the English-language textbook, and use it less and less. It is full of topics that are irrelevant, even cruel to Kosovar students:

Would You Like to Be a Millionaire?
Sister Wendy
Tourists in Your Country
Your Country's Factories and Businesses
Your First Car
Planning Your Retirement

And now today, the unit title is "National Stereotypes." This one, at least, would be more than appropriate, if I can find a good way to approach it. But the subject is full of snares and traps—full of land mines, to use a more local metaphor.

But I plunge ahead. We start with the stiff-upper-lipped Brit in his pub, the romantic Frenchman with his wine and his poodle, the tidy Dutch, the friendly Americans who value their jobs above all else. Are all Brits reserved? Are all Americans gregarious workaholics? No. We establish this.

Can stereotypes be harmful? I tell them about African Americans, the cruel stereotypes that helped keep them oppressed, and our national struggle to rid ourselves of these misleading pictures we used to justify our American apartheid.

And then—gulp!—we go to the Balkans. "What stereotype about Albanians do you think was used by Serbs to justify their oppression, the ethnic cleansing, the killing?"

Hands shoot up. "They say we are dirty." "They say we are stupid." "They say we have too many children." "They say we are lazy." "They say we are monkeys in the jungle."

I flinch as I hear this uncomfortable similarity to Jim Crow, but say nothing.

"And *are* all Albanians like that?" I ask, expecting their answer to make my point.

But there is a pause, and I see several students mulling this over. Uh-oh. This is going to be more complicated than I thought.

Finally Veton speaks. "Teacher, Albanians in *Kosova* are not like those things. But Albanians in *Albania*—yes. Many of these are dirty and lazy and criminals. They are not like us."

Vigorous head-nodding among some in the class.

I am stunned to hear from this intelligent student such damning generalizations about a large segment of his own ethnic group.

I am now very reluctant to ask the most important question. I want to know whether these students hate *all Serbs*. Do they think there is a good Serb anywhere in the world? Isn't that the ultimate question always? Whether one is capable of seeing the face in the crowd?

So I ask. How about Serbs?

They all want to speak, but Emina, her violet eyes blazing, gets there first. "Every one of them hates us, Teacher. They want to do terrible things to us."

"Don't you think that somewhere there are good Serbs, Serbs who don't hate you, didn't condone the killing?"

Silence now as they realize I am fishing for another answer. Luan clears his throat, as he always does when he has something important to say. "Teacher, we know you cannot say everyone is the same. Not all Americans. Not all British. But Serbs . . . the Serbs are all the same. They all want to kill us."

(In March 1999, Luan was in a room with several other male university students, when Serb police burst in. One held a gun to Luan's head as he and his friends were forced out and onto the trains, out of their country. He wrote an essay last month entitled "War Don't Like Nobody," and what it lacked in grammatical correctness, it more than made up for in drama.)

But my sense is that these young people are not voicing hate. They are voicing the certainty that they are hated. After all, it has been only a short time since the assassins were driven out of their country. They don't talk of wanting to kill Serbs—they talk of Serbs wanting to kill *them*. It is fear I am hearing.

I am in way over my head. Who can read another's heart? Who am I to try to teach tolerance to these who have suffered so much, so recently? I would feel more comfortable preaching against racial discrimination in the U.S., for I grew up in a small southern town in the '50s, believing all black people to be inferior and integration a sinful, dangerous thing. I know that evil from the inside out.

But here? I can understand nothing. Nothing except that the U.N. and the U.S. are foolish to think that Serbs and Albanians can live together peaceably anytime soon, that Kosovo Albanians will consent to being ruled by Serbia again. Albanians will never tolerate it. The fears, the suspicions, the memories, are both too recent and too deep.

FRIDAY, DECEMBER 1, 2000

Each time I go out of our house I realize I am not here just observing another culture. I am being observed, as well. I am acutely aware that my students see me not just as "Teacher," or "Paula," but as an *American,* a representative of my country. Every day, without trying and without realizing it, I am imparting American values and ideas. Whatever they see of me, hear from me, they will believe, "That is the way Americans are. That is what they think, that is how they act." It is a sobering thought.

"Why are you here?" I ask the class today. To attend English classes at this private school requires a financial sacrifice of their families, and a sacrifice of time and effort for the students. (After paying the $25 monthly tuition, Leonard's family has $105 to spend on everything else.) I want to get a sense of what they expect, what they need, what they want from this course.

They are happy to be asked, and the answer is simple: They know English is a key to a good education, a profitable career. Almost everyone would like to come to the U.S. to study, either for high school or university. (Although even here, in Kosovo, the word is out that U.S. students are lagging behind in math and science. My students feel they probably have better theoretical training in math and science than U.S. students do.) Many want to work in the U.S., at least for a time, to make money to send back to their families. Fazile has hopes of a career in economics and needs to speak English to advance in her profession. Drita wants to teach English, Luan and Faton need it for their graduate education and careers. For everyone, English is the passport to their future, and to the future of their families.

And here is the key distinction, I've found, between Kosovar students and American students: American students study in order to secure lucrative jobs and a sense of individual achievement. Kosovo Albanians study so they can provide for their families— their parents, siblings, and grandparents, as well as any future family they will have. Education is a family goal, not an individual goal.

Later...

Tonight I sit in bed with my journal marveling that I have continued to write in it almost every day since we got here. Despite decades of New Year's resolutions, I have never been able to consistently keep a diary. But here, for whatever reason, I am driven to write everything down as soon as possible. I don't want to forget anything or anyone. I don't want to muddle conversations in my memory. But mostly, I write because by writing I experience it all again, and begin to try to make some sense of it all.

Saturday, December 2, 2000

Again I meet the students in front of the school so I can walk them up Dragodan to our house for a meeting of the Hemingway Book Club of Kosova. Leutrim suggests we take a shortcut he knows about that will get us to the bottom of the hill more quickly. It *is* shorter, but wetter. We soon find the new route full of deep, wide mud puddles that the fifteen-year-old boys simply can't resist. As the older students and the girls watch scornfully, the daredevils attempt to jump the puddles—most landing smack in the middle, up to their ankles in muck. Good thing custom requires that people take off their shoes before entering a home. Igballe would faint seeing these shoes on her carpets!

We go directly up to the Red Salon. I offer cookies and juice, but most politely refuse. It is Ramadan, and they are fasting. (It is hard for adolescent boys to fast. Last week, as class drew to a close, Granit 2 burst from his chair, exclaiming, "I am sorry, Teacher, but I cannot wait any longer! It is dark now and I must eat!")

We browse through American magazines, one of their favorite occupations, and I let each of them choose a magazine to keep. Then we turn to *The Old Man and the Sea*. The reading this time has been difficult, they say. Granit 2, always a serious student, says he could use a vocabulary for the book—I promise to create one. Meanwhile, I've drawn pictures to help with some of the boating terms: "skiff," "gaff," "harpoon," "mast," "sail," "till."

We discuss the old man, his love of the sea and the creatures that live in it. Granit 2 says he reminds him of his own grandfather with whom he used to fish. But most of the students seem unable to relate to one of Hemingway's principal themes: our connection with the natural world. These are kids who have for most of their lives been confined to a grimy city where even the trees are littered with those thin, transparent plastic bags that so foul the streets. And the park outside of town is strewn not only with plastic bags and garbage, but with unexploded shells and land mines. The only animals these students see are the skeletal dogs and cats that scrounge the city's garbage piles. So when the old man speaks of the sea creatures as his "brothers," I see pleasure in the faces of my students, but little comprehension.

We read aloud the moment the old man hooks the fish:

> Just then, watching his lines, he saw one of the projecting green sticks dip sharply.
>
> "Yes," he said. "Yes," and shipped his oars without bumping the boat. . . . Then it came again. This time it was a tentative pull, not solid nor heavy, and he knew exactly what it was. One hundred fathoms down a marlin was eating the sardines that covered the point and the shank of the hook where the hand-forged hook projected from the head of the small tuna.

The old man waits, his hand cramping, his back aching, as the fish pulls him farther out to sea. But he doesn't see the fish until, after a long time,

> . . . he felt the difference in the pull of the line before he saw the slant change in the water. Then, as he leaned against the line and slapped his left hand hard and fast against his thigh he saw the line slanting slowly upward.
>
> "He's coming up," he said. "Come on hand. Please come on."
>
> The line rose slowly and steadily and then the surface of the ocean bulged ahead of the boat and the fish came out. He came out unendingly and water poured from his sides.

He was bright in the sun and his head and back were dark purple and in the sun the stripes on his sides showed wide and a light lavender. His sword was as long as a baseball bat and tapered like a rapier and he rose his full length from the water and then re-entered it, smoothly, like a diver and the old man saw the great scythe-blade of his tail go under and the line commenced to race out.

I wait for a while so Hemingway's words can paint a picture of the fish in their minds, then I show them the photograph I pulled off the web of a great marlin leaping from the sea.

"How can one old man in a tiny skiff hope to bring in such a great creature? Do you think he can do it?"

Without exception, they think he can. Yes!

"I will show him [the fish] what a man can do and what a man endures," the old man says.

We talk of the old man's persistence in the face of pain, fatigue, and suffering. Leutrim and Leonard say the old man reminds them of their Albanian hero, Skanderbeg, who spent twenty-five years fighting the Ottoman Turks. The comparison is more apt than the students yet know, for just as Skanderbeg fought a noble but ultimately losing battle to keep Albanian lands from being occupied by the Turks, so the old man will fail to bring to shore his big fish.

The students have frequently mentioned this fifteenth-century warrior. Most homes, including ours, boast a portrait of Skanderbeg. Ours (Igballe and Isa's) is embossed on a copper plate and hangs here in the Red Salon. In Kosovo, national heroes, even this fifteenth-century one, are not remote figures encountered only in history books as are our American heroes. Skanderbeg and his fellows are at the forefront of national consciousness and play a vital role in Kosovars' personal identity, in their pride as Albanians, and, I understand now, in their ability to endure what they have endured.

So how would you end this story if you were writing it? I ask. This question generates a lot of discussion. Genti would have the old man catch the biggest fish in the world and bring it back to Cuba to great acclaim and enormous wealth. Granit 2 would have the old man fall from the boat and, against all odds, swim all the way back to safety. Leutrim jokes that he would have the old man fall overboard and get eaten by sharks.

Well, I say, we'll read the rest of the book and find out. And next time I'll have the film. I've ordered it through the web and will pick it up when I'm back home in the States over Christmas. We'll actually *see* what happens.

I can tell they like the idea of the movie. So do I. Just hope I can get back to Prishtina with the video.

Tonight, lying in bed, Ed asks me to tell him every detail of the book club meeting, and I happily oblige.

SUNDAY, DECEMBER 3, 2000

Today Igballe spots my back brace. She pulls up her sweater and reveals her own brace. It's no good, though, she says. (We use a kind of sign language now that works well enough for most things.) She had a good one she had bought in London years ago, but the Serbs stole it when they looted the house.

Stole a *back brace*? Igballe did indeed lose everything.

MONDAY, DECEMBER 4, 2000

Luan tells me he's been invited by the university in Freiburg, Germany, to attend a two-week seminar in testing metals. He has brought me a copy of the invitation he was e-mailed yesterday. He is beaming, and looks like a prisoner who has just been given a reprieve. An opportunity! Such a rare thing here.

Halfway through the class the electricity goes off and we are plunged into darkness. In a few minutes one of the school staff comes in with two candles, one for each end of the long table. It is not enough light to read by, but I have an idea. The candle casts just enough light onto the white board behind me. I start making a series of hand-shadows on the board. "Rabbit!" cries Leutrim. "Duck!" And we take turns making the shadow animals, naming them in English and Albanian, laughing and (hopefully) still learning *something*. Anywhere else the situation might call for a "ghost story," but I decide these young people are already living with enough ghosts. We stick to the hand-shadows.

TUESDAY, DECEMBER 5, 2000

Faton is a very bright recent graduate in theoretical nuclear physics from the University of Prishtina. Although he is only twenty-two, his long face and anxious expression make him seem much older. He sits as close as possible to me in every class, as if physical proximity will facilitate the absorption of more English. He needs all the help he can get—his English is slow, halting.

He is desperate to continue his studies, and to do so in the U.S. or Western Europe. "There is no equipment here, Teacher. We have no computers. We never had much, and the Serbs stole what we had. I study old books only. It is all theory." He keeps saying to me, "I am young. And all I need is one chance. Just one chance. I will prove myself."

"Where did you and your husband go to college, Teacher?" he asks today. I tell him Ed went to Harvard and later got his master's and law degrees from the University of Virginia. I went to Lindenwood, a small women's college in Missouri, and got my master's degree in history at Southern Methodist University in Texas.

It is U.C. Berkeley that has fired his imagination—and the Lawrence Livermore Lab. But I'll never forget the look on his face when I told him the cost of tuition.

Today, he tells me he has applied for a job down at Camp Bondsteel, the huge American army base, as an interpreter. The job pays a thousand dollars a month. As a teacher he's making about $150 now. I offer to write a recommendation for him—yet I'm not sure his English is really good enough.

He knows he needs to make some money. He would agree with Leonard, who told me last week, "Teacher, I have learned there are two most important things. Health and money. And sometimes I think money is the most important."

Faton deserves his chance. I have never seen anyone more eager to study, to work. And today he tells me he wants to "give my contribution to America. To work for your country. You did very much for my country—you bring us freedom, you saved our lives. I consider it is our moral and national task to do good things for America." Like the others, Faton faces the obstacles of isolation, language, history, and his country's overwhelming poverty. But if anyone can make it, Faton can.

WEDNESDAY, DECEMBER 6, 2000

Twice a week Leonard and I stay after class for TOEFL tutoring. Today his friend Ardi has come with him to observe the reading comprehension exercises. The passages are long, complex, difficult, taken from actual tests. Leonard reads the text, then the first multiple-choice question. He sighs deeply and turns to me with a look of despair. He cannot even understand the question. The electricity suddenly goes out and we are in the dark. So the three of us turn to conversation.

I ask Ardi if he plans to attend university in Prishtina. No, not if I can help it, he tells me. Ardi, like many others here, believes that, as in the old Communist system, many teachers still consider themselves to be gods. They can be rude, unapproachable, and corrupt, selling grades for money or, sometimes, for sexual favors, he says. Having experienced corruption all their lives, Ardi and many of his generation are suspicious of people in places of power, like universities. He knows UNMIK is trying to clean up the university, but he is frustrated with their slow progress. He, like Leonard, will try to attend university in the U.S.

I tell them that they will both almost certainly need to start university in Prishtina, then try to transfer to a school in the U.S. later. I can't see Leonard's face clearly in the dark, but I can sense his disappointment. Leonard has seen the university's poor facilities, the library's bare shelves. He wants to believe in his country's institutions, especially the university system. But I can see he fears that Ardi may be right.

Yet, I am sure, attending college in Kosovo will be his only choice, at least for a while. How can I help Leonard accept that inevitability even as we seek his escape?

THURSDAY, DECEMBER 7, 2000

Our TV works most nights if the electricity is on. Everyone here has a satellite dish—thousands of huge white discs that make every house and apartment building look like a well-rigged ship ready to catch the breeze and sail away. We get costume dramas from Hungary, *Friends* overdubbed in Polish, flamenco dancing from Spain, soccer from Italy, soft porn from Turkey, local talent contests from Albania and Kosovo, and a host of unintelligible news programs from Egypt and Saudi Arabia. We don't watch narratives since we don't understand any of the languages, but we do enjoy the homegrown ethnic music and dancing. There are only three English-language stations—BBC World (all news), Eurosport (all sport), and Trinity Broadcast (all Jesus). I yearn for a movie or a *Seinfeld* episode.

Tonight we watched a few minutes of BBC news before the electricity went out. Now, we have our candles burning. I love the quiet that seems to permeate the house with their soft glow.

FRIDAY, DECEMBER 8, 2000
Peja, Kosovo

We're in Peja, or Pec in Serbian, a large town about two hours west of Prishtina. Ed, Sheryl, and Kate are training defense counsel in the conference room of our hotel. I am roaming the town. During March of 1999, almost every single Albanian was driven out of Peja, and much of the city was burned in an effort to make sure they would never return. This city of 100,000 people, the seat of the Serbian Orthodox Church, suffered greater damage than did any other sizable town in Kosovo except Gjakova. I hear it is beautiful country, mountains all around, but the fog is so thick today I can hardly see my feet, much less the mountains. The streets are muddy and as garbage-ridden as Prishtina. I walk blindly, trying to find the center of town. There are more country people here than one sees in Prishtina—old men and boys standing on wooden carts pulled by gaunt, tired horses with embroidered halters, farmers bent almost double under bulging bags of potatoes. They seem to emerge from the fog like ghosts.

Tonight as I sit in bed with my journal, thinking of the rape and murder, the looting and destruction of this historic, once beautiful town, I am overtaken by a sadness verging on depression. I will find it hard to sleep.

SATURDAY, DECEMBER 9, 2000

Ed comes back to the hotel room tonight laughing. "Who do you think really runs this country?" he asks me.

"Well, UNMIK, KFOR, OSCE . . . ," I say, though I know he has something else in mind.

"No, it's the *translators!*" he laughs. And taking off his sports coat he tells me the story: One of the participants at the training, a loud, loquacious attorney from Peja, was dominating the session this morning. He told long, boring stories unrelated to the subject at hand, and no one else, trainers or participants, could get in a word. Then the attorney got a cellphone call. He excused himself, went out onto the balcony, and the meeting resumed without him. When he returned, he once again seized the floor, but after a moment his cellphone rang again, so he excused himself and left. After this happened three times, he gave up trying to reclaim the floor.

Ed had thought the calls were simply fortuitous. But as he left the session he found the simultaneous translators at their hallway desk, still wearing their earphone/microphones, convulsed in laughter. Blerim, the head translator, held a cellphone. Fearing the attorney was about to disrupt the whole session, Blerim had simply given him a few anonymous calls!

Ed goes on to tell me of a contentious meeting in Prishtina last week where an Albanian judge and the French chair of the meeting started to get into a shouting match. One of our Kosovar friends was translating. When the Frenchman made insulting remarks about the judge's intelligence and education, our friend calmly translated, "The chair says it is time to adjourn for luncheon." Everyone duly left for lunch and later resumed their seats in a happier frame of mind.

SUNDAY, DECEMBER 10, 2000
Prishtina, Kosovo

Ed and I discuss the stress of being in Kosovo. It's not our old familiar American stress—the modern American syndrome of fast pace, overbooked schedules, frustrating commutes. Here, the very things that make the experience intriguing are the things that wear on our bodies and minds. We must be constantly alert, so that at the end of each day, no matter how satisfying the day may have been, we feel drained. It's as if our five senses are not enough. We must always use a sixth.

There are many reasons for this, we decide. Each encounter in the street or office is fraught with the potential for misunderstanding because of language difficulties and the deep cultural divide between us Americans and Kosovo Albanians. (What is the shopkeeper *really* thinking?) Each walk down any street takes us among heavily armed police or military, constant reminders of the danger, the potential for violence. Pedestrians compete with cars for the streets, the sidewalks, and the medians, so we're always dodging traffic as we walk. Deep pits, excavations in the road, are never fenced—I almost fell into one yesterday. We are always, even if unconsciously, making decisions about safety.

Then there is the pollution, the awful air and water and filthy streets, the mud or the dust—never anything in between—and the possibility of illness. And on a much more mundane note, we never know if we'll be able to get a bath this week or if I'll be able to cook dinner in the oven or will have to risk the gas-canister camp stove (it exploded last week). Or whether the house will be freezing or the cellphones will work or the satellite internet will be out.

And we live in an atmosphere of conflict, rumor, tension, suspicion—those fears and hatreds of the Kosovo Albanians for Serbs, of course. But there's also the unsettled nature of the foreign community and the jockeying for position and power of many organizations. There is more going on here than just the administration of aid to Kosovo. International politics are being played out in each committee meeting, each dinner conversation. Just being around these lonely, high-strung, exhausted people who have left their homes to work in Kosovo can be dispiriting.

There's the total incongruity of everyday life, starting with this very nice house so close to a mass grave of massacre victims, and the impossibly smiling faces of people who, we know, have just lived through hell. And then there's the surreal monolithic nature of the population. We never see Serbs, Roma, Turks, Gorani (Muslim Slavs), or any of the other ethnic and religious minorities who lived here for hundreds of years. Many of them have been driven out or underground in a kind of reverse ethnic cleansing, either by Albanians or, more often, by their own fear of Albanians. I can almost hear the cacophony of their various voices, almost feel their ghosts.

And finally there's our constant nagging worry: Are we really doing anything to help? Or are we just taking up space in an already overcrowded city?

I love it here. And to tell the truth, I even enjoy the challenge of living every day alert to that sixth sense. But it's not easy.

MONDAY, DECEMBER 11, 2000

The textbook, like all ESL texts, calls for the students to work in pairs on many exercises. Kosovo Albanians are clearly not prepared culturally for this. They may pair up, as instructed, turning their chairs slightly toward one another, but they will then continue to work separately.

Many Albanians, so the books have told me, are proud individualists, and they are fiercely competitive. Woe betide the student who makes a mistake reading aloud in class: "Wrong!" "Teacher, Teacher, that is not right! He made a mistake! I know the right answer!" Or in discussion, "Teacher, he has a silly idea! Let me tell you what *I* think!"

But it's all good-natured, and it always makes me laugh. "You have so many *opinions!*" I tell them today. They are delighted.

But tonight, as I write this, I wonder about this stubborn individualism, this independent streak. I remember Agim telling me everyone in Kosovo wants to be president. "We all want to be leaders," he told me. "There will be no followers!" If there is no tradition of cooperation and compromise for the common good, what chance do Kosovars have to govern themselves? What seems humorous in the classroom might well be a big problem for a future government.

TUESDAY, DECEMBER 12, 2000

I have found jars of Italian pesto! And at a small market in another part of town, inexplicably, two bottles of soy sauce. Now I feel I can cook.

I go to the butcher's. Because this is primarily a Muslim country, there is no pork in Prishtina, but calf and sheep carcasses hang in the windows of butcher shops, heads and all, dripping blood onto the floor so that I slip and slide up to the counter. There are no rump roasts or steaks or London broils. There are only large pieces and small pieces. So today I choose a small piece, which the friendly young butcher carefully wraps in white paper. Tonight I cut it into still smaller pieces and stir-fry it with some broccoli I found in an outdoor market on my way home. There were two stalks of broccoli—I snapped them both up, feeling like a wartime hoarder.

We don't have everything we want, but we can find almost everything we really need. Or we're able to improvise a suitable substitute. Or we've brought it from home. Like soft cotton sheets, prescription and over-the-counter medicines, Starbucks espresso.

Most people in this city, in this country, aren't living nearly as well as we are, and never will. What must they think of us foreigners living high on Dragodan Hill, away from the stench and confusion of downtown, in our large and, to them, luxurious houses?

WEDNESDAY, DECEMBER 13, 2000

Adem, the handsome high school senior with a small gold loop in his left ear (I haven't seen another in Kosovo), is usually quiet, attentive. But today he and Edona are agitated about something. They whisper and keep looking out the window. Then others start to look out the window. Finally, I stop trying to teach, and ask them what's going on.

"Look, Teacher! Look at the church! Look at the light!" They direct me so that I see the dome of the Serbian Orthodox church a few blocks away, and on top a large glowing cross. The cross has always been there. But now, for Christmas I guess, it looks as if someone has put lights on it so that it glows brightly, dominating the cityscape.

The students are incensed. "This is bad, Teacher." "They insult us, Teacher!" "It is too soon for this, Teacher!"

This has little to do with Islam. Though they are Muslim, there is no fanaticism in these students, and religion plays almost no part in Kosovo Albanians' politics. But they do see the Serbian Ortho-dox Church as the symbol, even an instigator of Serbian national-ism. So this outrage today is not about Serbs as Christians, but about Serbs as oppressors.

I call a break so they can go outside to see better, and as I look up from my desk I see Adem pacing, even more agitated, talking on his cellphone. He has called someone to tell him about the cross, about the insult. And it enters my mind: Is Adem, this dashing young man whose heroes are Che Guevara and former KLA leader Hashim Thaci, organizing an assault on the church? Of course not! But in Kosovo, I tell myself, one's mind seems to leap first to the craziest explanation for everything.

I'm reminded of this again tonight when I come home and Ed tells me it was merely the intense rays of a splendid sunset alighting on the golden cross that had caused it to glow this evening, stirring up passions among many in the city. Not Serbs. Not an insensitive UNMIK administration. Just a sunset.

THURSDAY, DECEMBER 14, 2000

Granit 2 tells me today before class that his uncle, who owns a cof-fee store by the old market, was told by KFOR troops to remove his poster of KLA heroes Adem, Shaban, and Hamza Jashari. Pic-tures of these men, a father and his two sons who, with fifty-five family members, were massacred in their homes by Serb police in 1998, are everywhere in Kosovo—in homes, shops, gas stations. The U.N. considers such pictures to be provocative, though, and tries to prohibit them. Granit, who translated the conversation for his uncle, is angy at what he perceives as a great injustice. "KFOR will be back tomorrow, Teacher. But my uncle, he says the picture will not come down."

FRIDAY, DECEMBER 15, 2000

Today it is home for the holidays. Leonard comes to our house this morning to say goodbye. He is carrying a box carefully wrapped with bright paper. "For you for your Christmas present," he says shyly. "From Nora and me." He wants me to open it now. It is a plastic music box in the shape of a grand piano. Its song is the theme from *Dr. Zhivago*. "I know you miss your piano, Teacher," Leonard says. "So Nora and I, we think maybe we will give you a piano for your Kosova home." I tell him, truthfully, that I have never received a gift that means so much to me.

Later . . .
Erol, a Turkish Macedonian taxi-company owner, has driven from Skopje and picks us up at our house at 10 a.m. to drive us back to Skopje where we will catch our plane. We have used Erol before for trips to Macedonia, and know that he has all the wheels and gears carefully oiled to get us through the border smoothly. He jokes with all the guards, and gives cans of orange Fanta to the passport offi-cials. As we pass through no-man's-land into Macedonia, he offers us his political commentary: "All Balkans are crazy! They all want bigger, bigger. Bigger Serbia, bigger Macedonia! But Albanish! They are craziest! Maybe Microsoft make them a new chip for here . . ."

and taps the back of his head. "Yes, that is what Albanish need, a new chip!"

MONDAY, JANUARY 8, 2001
Prishtina, Kosovo

We're back in Prishtina after a holiday in the U.S. Odd how I didn't have the impulse to keep my journal while I was home, but now that I'm back in Kosovo, it's the first thing I reach for. It's as if I know that my "real" life now is here. Even in the midst of family reunions in California, Arkansas, and D.C., I found my mind returning to my classroom, to the light-filled Red Salon where I plan my lessons and listen to Bulgarian choirs, to our comfortable bed with its growling tiger spread, even to the garbage-strewn steps down Dragodan.

And I think about how ironic it is that I am coming back to work in a country where the skills and experience of my lifetime—in historic preservation, environmental preservation, and marketing—are practically worthless. In Kosovo there is little cultural or natural heritage left to preserve, and not many products to sell, much less to "market." I am returning as a teacher, a thought that fills me with great happiness.

Today I show my students the things my friends at home have sent them. Liz, Donna, and Debbie gave me books, tapes, and visual aids for the classroom. I loaded up on more school supplies in D.C. before flying back. Today I pass the goodies around the table and write my friends' names on the board. They are now a part of our class.

"Thank them for us, Teacher," says Fazile, and everyone nods happily.

I look around. Everyone is here today, eager to get back to work.

Drita, whose hair was long when I left for vacation, sports a new, fashionable bob. "Very becoming, Drita!" Luan is looking ruggedly handsome in his black leather jacket; Edona, whose mother is Catholic, wears her Christmas present, a new orange sweater; Faton, as usual, has chosen the chair to my left, and has organized his notes and books neatly in front of him; the Granits, Besart, Genti, and Leutrim—the fifteen-year-old boys—sit next to each other to share notes and chat; Leonard is quiet, as always, but looks very happy, and Emina and Fatmira chatter and beam at me: "We've missed you, Teacher!"

After class, as always, I take a taxi back up Dragodan to get home. A long line of drivers waits outside the stadium/shop complex housing the school. As far as I can tell, anyone can be a taxi driver. Just put a sign on your car and you're in business. The cars are all small and shabby. The drivers, invariably, are friendly and polite. I'm on chatty terms with several, though I know them only by their eyes in the rearview mirrors. Most speak a few words of English. One driver, whose English is fairly good, told me he learned it from listening to American pop music on his car radio.

Tonight I have a new driver, a gaunt dark young man, who tells me he has just gotten out of prison. I know immediately he means he is one of those arrested or captured by Serb forces during the war. International pressure has just forced Serbia to release hundreds of these prisoners. He was there for eighteen months he says, and was beaten almost every day. "All my . . ." He points to his side. "Ribs," I supply. "Yes, ribs, broke."

How did you survive such treatment, I ask? There is a pause as he thinks this over.

Finally, "Some men are hard as stones."

Yes, I am back in Kosovo.

TUESDAY, JANUARY 9, 2001

At 3 p.m. precisely, Leonard rings the doorbell, here for his tutorial. We have decided to work together for three hours every Tuesday and Thursday. Today we use the audiotapes for listening comprehension—long dialogues which Leonard listens to intently, then answers multiple-choice questions about. The dialogues are difficult enough, but the questions are what stump him. He simply doesn't have the vocabulary to understand them.

This despite the fact that, while I was in the U.S. over the holidays, Leonard, on his own initiative, put together a list of three thousand English words—the most frequently used words in English according to the dictionary I gave him last fall—and has begun defining them in both English and Albanian. Today he shows me this vocabulary notebook, each word neatly, painstakingly printed.

The TOEFL is in less than two weeks, and the SAT, a test we don't have time to even think about much less prepare for, is in three weeks. We have started to talk about how this extra English he's learning will help him throughout his life in innumerable ways, not just as preparation for the TOEFL. We have started, in other words, trying to prepare each other for defeat.

WEDNESDAY, JANUARY 10, 2001

Faton has brought his physics professor with him. He is a handsome, dignified gentleman of about fifty with carefully combed gray hair, glasses, a wool tweed suit, knit vest and tie. In a formal but friendly way, he asks if I might find room for him in the class. "Please forgive me for coming late to your class. I have only now

heard of it from my student, Faton. I hope you will permit . . . ?"
Yes, of course, I tell him. Welcome. Though I secretly wonder how
this older, very distinguished-looking professor will fit into this
class of young people. Will he be bored? Will the younger students
be intimidated, lose their spontaneity?

Each day I hand out materials I brought from the U.S. and have
had copied for everyone. Feature articles, cartoons that illustrate
points of grammar, diagrams, charts, and lists. By now each student
is beginning to build quite an English-language library. Today I
hand out timelines my ESL school in San Francisco gave me: Present simple: I do. Present continuous: I am doing. Past simple: I did.
Past continuous: I was doing. Future: I will do/I am going to do.
Future continuous: I will be doing. And so forth. These materials
are invaluable supplements to the scanty materials available here in
Kosovo. And God knows they are invaluable to me! I spend each
evening reviewing them, trying to remind myself of the fine points
of grammar I haven't thought about in thirty years. I sometimes
feel I'm staying only a day ahead of the class.

THURSDAY, JANUARY 11, 2001

Leonard's conversational English has improved so much. When I
first met him last fall, he could hardly put three words together.
Now he chatters away confidently. Well, a slow chatter. But then,
Leonard speaks Albanian slowly, thoughtfully. It is his way.

He is struggling to keep his spirits up in the face of almost certain disappointment with the TOEFL. "I have not lucky in my life,"
he says. Leonard is a great believer in luck, probably because he's
not had much of it that's good.

I rummage around on my desk for my copy of *The Old Man and the Sea* and find the passage I want. "Remember this? The old man says 'It is better to be lucky. But I would rather be exact. Then when luck comes you are ready.' Hemingway is telling us that it's good to have luck, but becoming skillful, learning, trying hard is even better. You must do your best so you can be ready when the luck comes."

Leonard smiles politely, but cannot muster much enthusiasm today.

After our TOEFL review, we sit together at my desk in the Red Salon and I show him pictures of Monument Valley and Canyonlands, of Yosemite and Point Reyes National Seashore. He is awed. "I cannot believe it, Teacher. So much beauty in one country!" He is thoughtful for a moment. "Once when I was little, my parents took me to a place outside Prishtina where water came up out of the ground." "A spring," I offer. "Yes," he says wistfully. "A spring. It was the most beautiful thing I have ever seen."

FRIDAY, JANUARY 12, 2001

The Professor—he calls me "Mrs. Paula" and I call him "Professor"—has a deep, beautiful voice that resonates through the class as he consults with Faton, trying to keep up. He has a natural dignity and sophistication, but also has a gleam in his eye, a quick smile, and a wonderful sense of humor. He seems right at home in this class of much younger people, and already I can see the other students warming to him.

Tonight, Ed, Sheryl, Kate, and I skid through the icy streets to have dinner at the Indian restaurant. Somehow, in the hush of this snowy evening, Kosovo seems more lonely, more cut off than ever from the rest of the world. We treasure the company of these dear American friends tonight.

SATURDAY, JANUARY 13, 2001

Today I sit and muse: It's not as easy physically to be here at age fifty-six as it might have been, say, at age thirty. My back hurts most of the time. My eyesight bothers me. My memory isn't as good as it was and my reflexes seem to have slowed down.

But psychologically, emotionally, I think I am handling it better now than I might have at thirty. For one thing, I'm too old to be sure of much anymore, which is just as well. It wouldn't do to be in Kosovo with too many certainties or convictions. I am able to be simply *present* now. I listen more, talk less. And at age thirty I think I might have been fixated on trying to *achieve* something. At age fifty-six I just feel open to what presents itself.

SUNDAY, JANUARY 14, 2001

The snow is thick on the ground, covering up most of the garbage, muffling the sounds of gunshots and generators. It is possible to imagine tonight that this is a pure place, an innocent land where nothing bad ever happened, where nothing bad could happen.

Ed walked up the street a few minutes ago to the U.S. Mission to meet with Senator Joseph Biden. He is one of a small group of Americans who've been asked to brief the senator on what's being done and what needs to be done about Rule of Law issues.

And there *are* issues. The only legal experience local judges and attorneys have had was with the old Communist system. None of the Kosovo Albanian lawyers were permitted to practice during the '90s, the decade of apartheid. They are woefully undereducated and inexperienced, and it's the international community's job to train them. Yet the trainings themselves are ridiculously inadequate, Ed says. Last week's judicial training in which Ed taught was originally scheduled to take four days. But the sponsor, OSCE, whittled it down to three and finally to two days. Ed said they might as well grind up the training materials and feed it to the judges in capsules.

And many critical materials aren't available in Albanian. Ed is supposed to be training judges and attorneys in the European Convention on Human Rights. But he discovered last week that none of the case law, that body of law that interprets and makes sense of the Convention, has been translated into Albanian.

And then there are the salaries. How can a legal system be constructed when UNMIK pays local judges only $300 to $400 a month, an amount guaranteed to foster bribery and corruption? (International judges brought in to hear cases earn about $10,000 a month.) So what can Ed do? What can *anyone* do to establish a legal system here?

Like many internationals trying to help Kosovars, Ed alternates between hope and despair. But he perseveres, and I'm so proud of what he's doing. The Rule of Law, a legal system in which just laws apply equally to everyone, is surely one of the West's most valuable exports to Kosovo. It is the foundation on which a lasting peace must be built. But it is no panacea, and it is not something in which people easily believe.

MONDAY, JANUARY 15, 2001

Down to the national theater for an evening of traditional Albanian folk song and dance. The microphone is too loud, and screeches and squawks through much of the female soprano's numbers. But the Eagle Dance, in which two dashing young men dressed as eagles swoop and soar together all over the stage, is powerful, magnificent. As I clap and smile, utterly delighted with the performance, the young woman next to me says, "You like our Albanian music, yes?" *"Po! Po!"* I tell her. "It's wonderful!" She is very pleased.

TUESDAY, JANUARY 16, 2001

The TOEFL is less than a week away. I see today, with certainty, that Leonard cannot possibly make a high score. He simply started too late. He knows it, too. At the end of our session he looks at me and says, "Teacher, I am afraid that if I fail the TOEFL, you will be sad." I tell him I don't have enough English words to tell him how proud I am of him! He passed *my* test long ago simply by trying. And I remind him of what I've said often the last few months: His acing the TOEFL so soon, after so little English training, is a long shot.

Then we talk about the parable of the tortoise and the hare. "Slow but steady wins the race." He brightens a bit. He knows this parable, too. "You have just started the race, Leonard. And you must be prepared to be steady for a long time."

He nods. "Patience."

"Yes," I say, "that's the right word."

"But you know, Teacher?" he says finally, refusing to be comforted. "I don't think my story will have an American ending."

WEDNESDAY, JANUARY 17, 2001

I've asked the class to write short essays on their experiences after Serbia started the military crackdown in March 1998, and have given them an alternative subject if, for any reason, they don't wish to write about the war. Most have written about what happened to them in the spring of 1999, after NATO started to drive the Serbs out.

BESART: A tall, gangly fifteen-year-old with reddish hair and a perpetually worried expression. Bright, shy, a football (soccer) player. I have to scold him sometimes to keep him from talking out of turn. Besart! Hush! In the spring of 1999, he and his family were forced by Serb paramilitaries to walk 32 kilometers out of town. When they returned, their house had been burned, everything they owned stolen or destroyed.

GRANIT 1: My scamp, the kid for whom the word "mischievous" was invented. Wiry black hair and vivid azure eyes. I notice today he is looking over Besart's shoulder. "Where is your textbook, Granit?" He stutters around. "I dropped it, Teacher, in the muddy water." The class roars. I laugh, too. It is so typical of this kid. There's no chance, of course, he can afford another one. We will improvise.

Like Leonard, Granit and his family hid out in their apartment during the three-month bombing, suffering the special terror of the trapped. Today, typically, he has forgotten to write his essay. As I collect the papers from the rest of the class, he grins at me sheepishly, and I grin at him. Granit! Not again!

Granit 1 told me last week that he wasn't as frightened as the rest of his family during the ethnic cleansing. "I knew NATO would save us," he said, smiling.

GRANIT 2: Though his manner is typically serious, somber even, Granit 2 has a great sense of humor and a lively, curious mind. He is one of the smartest kids in the class and the most enthusiastic member of the Hemingway Book Club of Kosova. He loves rock and roll, but also classical music. I believe he has the heart of a poet, or of a composer.

When the Serbs came to roust his family out of their house, he took one last look back into his room, he writes, fearing he would never see his books and his music again. "My eyes had no tears, but

I cried in my heart." He and his family joined the thousands of Albanians who walked, "crying and moaning," past burning houses to the trains. "Some of the people appeared in the train windows and I could see their faces were wet from the crying." After he returned from the refugee camp months later, everything had gone up in smoke. "But we built again our home," he writes, "and we live together in peace and freedom."

As I recount this tonight in my journal, I marvel at how quickly Kosovo is being rebuilt. Yes, there is international help, a lot of it. But it is the Kosovars themselves who set the pace. After NATO drove the Serb army out in June 1999, the Albanian refugees were told to wait in their camps until they could be returned in an orderly way. But nothing could stop these people. They surged back over the border into Kosovo by the hundreds of thousands, returning to their devastated towns as fast as they could go, getting back to what was left of their lives. Clearly, that is what my students and their families did.

EMINA: Before Emina, her mother, aunt, and brother fled Prishtina, she got out her makeup kit and drew lines on her beautiful face and smudges beneath her violet eyes to try to look old. She covered her lustrous black curly hair with a shawl and dressed as an old woman. She told her brother, seventeen and with a mind of his own, not to be defiant, not even to look interested in his surroundings, but simply to lean on her as if he was crippled and, maybe, simple. They had waited too long to leave Prishtina with most of the other Albanian refugees, so the bus they got on was a commercial bus headed south toward Macedonia. There were three Albanian families on the bus including hers; the rest were Turks and Serbs.

They were stopped at one point by a group of armed paramilitaries. The leader's face was painted in the patterns of camouflage, but the paint, Emina says, was blood. He waved a large curved knife covered with blood, and demanded to know of the bus driver, who was a Serb, if there were any Albanians aboard. "The driver knew we were Albanian," said Emina. "But he told the Serb paramilitaries that we were all Serbs on the bus. He felt sorry for us, I guess. He saved our lives."

The driver, apparently fearing for his own life, stopped the bus a few miles down the road and asked the Albanian families to get out. They spent the next few nights hiding in the brush, living "like animals," exposed to the cold, eating and drinking only the little they had with them. After a few days a mother of three young children, a woman who had been ill when they left Prishtina, died. "The cold was too much for her," Emina says, "and the fear. We knew we must leave so we buried her as much as we could, took her children, and went to the road again." They were picked up by another bus driver who took them to the camps at the Macedonian border where they stayed for several weeks, placing their names on the list to be evacuated to whatever country would take them. They wound up as refugees in Australia, where Emina's brother remains.

DRITA: Drita's voice is almost a whisper, but she has overcome her shyness enough to participate in class. Her conversational English is improving rapidly. She always does her homework, attends every extra conversation class, and hopes to attend university and teach English.

She and her family live in a village outside of Prishtina. In the early days of the war, she says, the people in her village had been troubled by mysterious gunfire coming from a village not far away. They soon discovered that the shots were of the massacre by Serb paramilitaries of many civilians, including old people, women, and children. "We were very shocked and terrified," she writes, "and thought it might happen to us."

Before NATO started bombing, Serb police "were everywhere

in the streets of my village. They were very aggressive and their behavior was very bad." She and her siblings stopped going to school and her parents stopped going to work. They hid in their home, not knowing "if we would be killed, like so many other people. Sometimes I tried to read my book, but I couldn't concentrate on it, so I left it and just waited."

Then, three weeks after the NATO bombing began, the Serb army came to her village and told them all to leave. " 'Go wherever you want,' " they said, " 'This is Serbia's land, and if you don't leave by tomorrow you will all be killed.' "

Drita and her family fled, first to a Macedonian camp, then as refugees to England, where they stayed for the duration of the war. When they came back, their house had been destroyed, everything lost. "My father built it again," she writes, simply.

I picture this gentle young woman sitting anxiously in her room, her unread book on her lap, listening for the sounds of more gunshots or the banging on the door, and I want so much to be able to take that memory away from her, to somehow give her a secure *past* as well as a secure future.

EDONA: At fifteen, Edona is beautiful with olive complexion, long, light brown hair, and large, carefully made-up eyes. Were she in the U.S., her face would dominate teen fashion magazines. Although all the students dress neatly, Edona's wardrobe suggests a more affluent household than most. She lives with her family on Dragodan Hill. She is bright, poised, and self-confident. She has had many private English classes and speaks the language well.

In an earlier essay about career goals, she said she used to want to be a doctor, but that "now I don't like this profession because I've understood that if I would be a doctor I would have to spend all my life with sick people." So now she wants to be an architect, with, presumably, a healthier clientele.

In today's essay she writes that she and her family were routed out of their house by Serb police. When they returned, everything had been stolen by Serb forces, and friends and family members were missing. It took months for Edona to feel safe again, she says, and to find that all their family were safe in various camps and countries.

LEUTRIM: Another bright fifteen-year-old. Blond, cute, witty, gregarious. He and his family wound up with official refugee status, staying six months in New Jersey with relatives. The extended family, Leutrim told me last week, lived on money his uncle was getting from some rich American named "Wolfar." The whole family, including the newly arrived refugees, worked at whatever jobs they could find, but their combined income wasn't enough to live on. "And if we made too much money, Wolfar wouldn't give us any more of *his* money!"

"Ah!" I suddenly understood. *"Welfare!"*

When they returned to Kosovo, Leutrim's father, an accountant, had lost his job. Now, a year and a half later, he and his wife, an attorney, are still unemployed.

LUAN: A graduate mechanical engineer, Luan writes: "The war don't like nobody. It comes always without wishes of people who feel it the most dreadful. Nobody can't know better than Albanian people of Kosova what is violence, what is killing people and nobody can't hate it more than they. They are afraid of repetition massacres."

At thirty, Luan remembers well the years of apartheid, when the Serb government brutally cracked down on Kosovo Albanians, depriving them of jobs, education, medical care, basic civil rights. He describes how terrified he and fellow Albanians were just walking down the streets. He was coming home from class one day, he writes, when three "hunters," Serb policemen in civilian clothes, stopped them. "Who is the president of Serbia?" they asked. "Who is prime minister?" Luan knew the first answer but not the second. "I felt a terrible ache in the back of my head and I fell down. The policeman agent continued to hit me even though I was lied down and almost lost my mind [became unconscious]. They did the same thing to my friend." He continues in the way most Albanians relate their stories, by writing that "compared with some other cases that happened to many of my friends, my case is not so important to talk about. Many students got mental problems and they had to stop the studies. This is a short story of the long ethnocide that the Serbian regime made to Kosovars."

Later, during the ethnic cleansing, he writes, he was herded at gunpoint onto the cramped, airless train with thousands of others, and found himself dumped in Bllaca, the hellish no-man's-land between Kosovo and Macedonia where there were no tents, no toilets, no food, no medical care. Many died in the first cold nights before aid arrived. "The best producer in Hollywood," Luan writes, "could not make such terrible scenes. Here all people were transformed to poor people. They had been intellectuals, artists, businessmen . . . but now they were only poor people who ran for a piece of bread."

As all my students remind me in these essays, Prishtina suffered far fewer murders than did the rest of the country. Here in the capital it was mostly the leaders who were killed—politicians, lawyers, human rights activists, intellectuals, and, of course, those who were suspected of being KLA. It was the rural areas that constituted the killing fields. The Serb army and paramilitaries swept through the countryside destroying farmhouses, villages, and towns, killing many of the people in them. The official count is ten thousand dead, though Albanians say there were many more. Almost all my students lost family members in the countryside, but because they lived in the city, none of these students lost parents or siblings.

FATON: Faton was nineteen when the bombing started, and lived in a small town. He writes:

> When the first NATO freedom-strikes began, it was the most happy moment for Kosovars because we saw that the reality is going to be changed. In that night began an enormous shooting from Serbs and Roms. During that night they firstly stole and then burnt nearly all Albanian shops (including markets for food supply). At the same time they began shooting with snipers and automatic guns. It was *fear!!!*
>
> During that time I was with my family and with some of my neighbors listening to the news in a small radio (with batteries), and waiting what is going to happen. On the second day I saw many villagers from some of the villages around my town coming to find the safety place because the army and paramilitary forces were invaded in their houses. It was a chaos—everybody was moving as without a head, children crying and screaming, people shooting—it was a real *hell.*
>
> As the days passed the number of people in town who was taken from their families and executed began to rise. Then I with my family and some neighbors went to a village ten kilometers from my town. There was no other choice, just to move to where we believed there is safety. We were unarmed, we just waited until somebody would come to kill us—it was fear—no hopes that somebody would save us—but the worstest thing that every male person thought was: What if somebody will massacre us in front of our women and children—it was a real *hell.*
>
> We stayed four days in this village. After the third day there the Serb forces invaded some of the neighboring villages and forced people to leave their houses. There were

many victims killed in front of their families. People from those villages, children, old people . . . came in my village and told us. We expected that our village will be next, so my family with some others went back into our town. [At that moment the only hope for life was to move from one place to the other.] Two days after, the Serb forces invaded that village.

We stayed in my town a couple of days but not in my home because one day while we were in the village some civilian Serbs asked some refugee children about my father. We didn't know the reason, but what we know was that this search for him is not a good sign. And we were right. One colleague of my father and also a neighbor was taken by Serbs and killed.

The food was at the end, during the night and days there were a lot of shootings. The streets were empty. No people, no children playing, even no dogs and cats. Serb snipers were positioned in the neighboring houses (50 to 100 meters distance from my home) where they were shooting at whatever was human. They destroyed one house and killed the owner with explosives.

We didn't have any choice but to leave our home and go to the train station. My family and I stayed in a camp in Macedonia and finally went as refugees to Turkey for three months. But we were very lucky (thank *god*) that nobody didn't separate in the train station and during the travel because there was many cases when the people were separated (mans from the womens and children and nobody doesn't know until now where they are).

Faton ends his essay as his fellow students from Prishtina ended theirs, saying he was very lucky.

Thursday, January 18, 2001

In conversation practice after class today we discuss families. They want to know about American teens. What do they do after high school? I tell them that when American kids graduate from high school they usually leave home to attend college or to work in a distant place. And after college, often, their work may be many miles, perhaps thousands of miles away from their parents, their hometown. It is modern life in America.

The class are stunned. "They leave their *families?*" Luan says, incredulous. Genti looks almost hurt by the news. "Why do they want to leave their mothers and fathers?" he asks.

In some cases it's necessary to leave in order to get a good education, I explain.

"But why don't they come home after college?" Silvete asks. She is a buxom twenty-one-year-old blonde with blue eyes whose close-fitting sweater shows lots of creamy cleavage. "I could never leave my mother and my sisters!" she declares.

They are shocked to discover that I live two thousand miles away from my parents.

I remind them that almost every Albanian family has at least one family member working somewhere in Western Europe.

"Yes, but they go to Germany or Italy because they *must,* so they can send money home to their families," Luan explains. "Every Albanian wants to come back home to his family. And when they make enough money, they *will* come home."

Family is everything to Albanians. It is the image, the structure that makes sense of everything else. It is why, I think, Jehona thinks of Ed and me as "Mom and Dad," why Leonard calls me his "American Mom," why Bajrum, the little sunflower seed salesman, adopted us in the sports stadium. In Kosovo, parents constantly hug and stroke and caress their children. Children, *teenagers,* love their mothers and fathers. They do not feel entitled to demand, to misbehave, to argue with or terrorize their parents. My students frequently tell me how grateful they are to their parents, how much they love them. "My father gives me the best advices," Leonard says. "My mother is my best friend."

What are we Americans doing wrong?

FRIDAY, JANUARY 19, 2001

It is impossible to comprehend how limited the lives of Kosovo Albanians are, to understand the extent of their insularity, their ignorance of the world. I get a glimpse of this again today when, as I illustrate a point of grammar by passing out color photographs taken from American magazines, I see the reactions of my students: "Where did you get these pictures, Teacher!" "These are beautiful, Teacher!" The pictures—a *National Geographic* baboon, a Jewish synagogue in Jerusalem, Tony Blair, a slinky fashion model, the Olympic runner Marion Jones, a modern kitchen—which I thought of as merely the most pedestrian of visual aids, are thrilling for these students.

Yes, they see American movies and television programming on their TVs, but they have very little sophisticated reading material from the outside world. Even if they could afford it, there is little published here in their language. Much of the world's literature, past and present, is inaccessible to these Kosovar Albanians. And their Albanian-language newspapers cover mostly local events. Only a few magazines show life in the greater world. Many of these young people have never traveled outside the country and, apart from me, know no one from outside the Balkans. The walls that surround them are high and close in. They cannot see beyond their own provincial town.

As they pore over the photographs, I am suddenly filled with a certainty that what I am doing here, teaching English, is a good thing. Not that I think that the English language represents a superior culture. No. We are learning from *each other* how best to live. Rather, it's that the class, by its very nature, is cosmopolitan. It opens for these students a window onto the world, a world they must understand if they are to thrive, if they are to live without violence. Or, to try another metaphor, it creates a crack in the thick walls of their isolation. Just as being here in Kosovo, being with these students, has created a crack in the walls of my own isolation. And who knows, through these cracks a little light might flow—for all of us.

Later...

Tonight I am reading again from Rebecca West's 1941 *Black Lamb and Gray Falcon,* probably the best book ever written on the Balkans. Of Luccheni, the impoverished, unemployed assassin of Empress Elizabeth of Austria, West says:

> Many people are unable to say what they mean only because they have not been given an adequate vocabulary by their environment, and their apparently meaningless remarks may be inspired by a sane enough consciousness of real facts. . . . [Luccheni] said with his stiletto to the symbol of power: "Hey, what are you going to do with me?" He made no suggestions, but cannot be blamed for it. It was the essence of his case against society that it had left him unfit to offer suggestions, unable to form thoughts or design actions other than the crudest and most violent.

The people of Kosovo—Albanians, Serbs, Roma, Gorani, Bosniaks, and all the rest—must be given an "adequate vocabulary" to express their fears, frustrations, angers, desires, and ambitions in ways other than violence. Education can provide that vocabulary. Without it, the future itself is hopeless.

SATURDAY, JANUARY 20, 2001

It's impossible to have a conversation with a Kosovar in which the subject of history doesn't eventually take over. The ancient Illyrians, the medieval Serb kingdoms, Skanderbeg and Prince Lazar, the Ottoman Empire, the Balkan Wars, the World Wars, Tito—and of course, the tragedies of the past decade. It is this history, they believe, that explains what has happened to them, that describes who they are. It is always on their minds.

The trick, of course, is to distinguish history from myth—and Kosovo is full of myths, both Serbian and Albanian. For this reason I keep our history books—Malcolm, Kaplan, Mertus, Judah—close at hand. These journalists and historians help me sort out truth and myth, provide some perspective.

This week Leonard told me about the "poisoning of the students." In March and April of 1990, he says, Albanian students in Prishtina's segregated schools started to get sick. Thousands of them were passing out, having difficulty breathing, experiencing nausea and stomach pain. Rumors spread quickly and it was soon believed by most Albanians that the students had been poisoned by Serbs, either with a nerve gas or some other chemical. Serb counterrumors argued that the children were simply victims of mass hysteria, or that, if they were indeed ill, they were victims of an Albanian plot to discredit Serbs. Leonard contends the poison was put by Serb teachers into letters addressed to Albanian students and placed into baskets for them to open. The poison, he says, made his aunt very sick, and made others mentally ill.

"Imagine, Teacher," he said, "that teachers poisoned their own students!"

That night I looked in our books for the "poisoning of the students." And the truth, as always in Kosovo, is very complicated. Thousands of children were indeed taken to hospitals, and tests were conducted by Albanian, Serb, and international doctors and scientists. Many U.N. observers felt mass hysteria was the only culprit; yet, a toxicologist from the U.N. and a study conducted by a Belgian lab concluded that nerve gas, either sarin or tabun, was present in the blood of some of the children. Serbs contend the studies were biased, but never allowed a comprehensive international investigation to take place.

The truth, as Julie A. Mertus concludes in *Kosovo: How Myths and Truths Started a War*, will never be agreed upon by both Serbs and Albanians. But for Leonard, as for many Albanians, the "poisoning of the students" is a historical truth, another tragic incident in the victimization of Kosovo Albanians.

SUNDAY, JANUARY 21, 2001

At dinner tonight, over beef and pasta soup (cooked over our camp stove), canned pears, and candlelight, Ed discusses the pleasures and the frustrations of his week. The greatest frustration, which he is still fuming about, came at the Judicial Advisory Committee meeting Thursday. The committee is supposed to advise UNMIK about law. This week Ed recommended that the committee advise UNMIK to provide help for those who were psychologically traumatized by the war—rape victims, families of murder victims, soldiers—any who suffer from post-traumatic stress disorder. Isn't a woman who was gang-raped as much in need of help as someone who was shot in the shoulder? If the gunshot victim can be given medical attention, couldn't the rape victim be offered psychological counseling?

But it soon became clear, Ed says, that the committee's function in this case was primarily to rubber-stamp UNMIK's rules and actions, not to recommend new ones. Ed and some of his colleagues lodged an indignant protest. Never, Ed told the committee, has he seen a veterans' or victims' rights program—and he has worked on several—that did not offer help for those whose minds have been wounded.

Ed paces the floor of the Red Salon tonight, over to the window and back to the door. His face is full of frustration, despair. It is an issue that means a lot to him, and he feels the cause, for the moment anyway, is lost. He is still distraught when we get into bed. I rub his shoulders and back, hoping he can sleep.

MONDAY, JANUARY 22, 2001

Before class, I ask Leonard how the TOEFL went on Saturday. "It was too hard, Teacher. Every student who took it said it was too hard. I am sure I did not pass." But he is clearly glad it is over; he had been so worried. We have done all we can do, for now.

Later . . .
Tonight, as I read and correct grammar in some of my students' essays, I am struck by the eloquence of their simple stories. And it occurs to me that in some ways their prose resembles Hemingway's.

Hemingway told his stories in short, unadorned sentences. The strength of his meaning emerged as much from what he didn't say as from what he did say. This famously terse, taut style of writing has, of course, over the years provoked as much scorn and parody as it has praise, but I rather agree with Ford Maddox Ford, whose opinion of Hemingway's prose I found on the web yesterday. Hemingway's words, said Ford, are "like pebbles fetched fresh from the brook."

In my students' case they leave words out because they must. They simply haven't the vocabulary to express the subtleties of their feelings, or to describe with detail and precision what they see.

Leonard writes of seeing a televison interview with local families whose sons/brothers/fathers/husbands are still missing—either dead or perhaps in Serbian jails somewhere. "I cried to listen to them," he writes. "Their words attacked my heart." Granit 2 writes that when the Serbs were driving Prishtina residents from the city, the road in front of his house "looked like a snake, moving." When he and his family joined the exodus, he looked into houses along the way where he saw "people in the middle of fire."

I think the power of their language is that it speaks to the very incomprehensibility of the experiences they are trying to describe. Their sparse language, and even their misuse of words, draws the reader's attention to the fact that there are some things no skill with vocabulary—and no perfectly chosen combination of words—can come close to capturing. There are times when we can only speak in fragments.

People in the middle of fire. Simple, clear, vivid. Hemingway-esque.

Tuesday, January 23, 2001

Today Leonard and I go over the SAT format—how to fill in his name and personal information, how the test is structured, and how to mark the answers. Although I had found an SAT prep book for him last November, he has had time only to discover that he can't understand all the questions. I think he could do the math if the questions and instructions were in Albanian.

We're both pretty fatalistic about this test. It will be this Saturday.

WEDNESDAY, JANUARY 24, 2001

I have been feeling awful. Sinus infection. The antibiotics I brought from home aren't making a dent. Today the Professor, aware that I've been ill, brings me a jar of his homemade . . . we search for a word and settle on "syrup." He made it especially for me, he says, and it is particularly good for head congestion. He describes in detail how he made it, crushing the grapes, boiling the juice, adding no sugar, making sure it didn't ferment—"There is no alcohol, Mrs. Paula!" The secret lies in what you do to the grapes, he says. He has wrapped it in newspaper, and hands it to me with some ceremony, as if it is a magic potion. I hope it is.

It's a great day in class. I ask Fazile if she would like some help with "business English"—business letters, forms, etc. We resolve to work together on practical things she can use in her job. And I hand out articles I've cut from English-language newspapers and magazines: For Besart, the soccer news; for Genti, American basketball; for the Professor, a review of a new book on physics; for Drita, an article on Mel Gibson's newest movie (she has a crush!); for Fatmira and Emina, an article I got from the web on Mother Teresa, the Roman Catholic nun who is a heroine to these Muslim girls.

Thursday, January 25, 2001

The Professor's potion must be working. I feel well enough to go out, even though the snow is deep, a thick layer of ice under it, and the weather is frigid. I bundle up in my heaviest down, pick up my stacks of books and papers, and head down Dragodan to school. The steps, treacherous even in dry weather when you can *see* them, are today almost certain disaster. And sure enough, on the fifth step down, my feet fly out from under me and I land *Plop!* square on my rear, bouncing down a few more steps, my books and papers flying downhill. Cushioned by layers of down, I don't feel a thing, get up and try it again. Another few steps and *Plop!* Harder this time, but I hang on to my books and still, feel nothing. I look up and see several little boys—seven-year-olds probably—looking at me in bewilderment, wondering, no doubt, what the proper reaction should be to this very clumsy foreign lady. Then, seeing that I am laughing so hard I can hardly breathe, the little guys start to giggle. One comes over and helps me to my feet. We shake hands all round and I continue down the hill, feeling exuberant, like a child in the snow.

Friday, January 26, 2001

Silvete brings her seven-year-old niece to class. The little girl sits quietly throughout the class, thoroughly charming and well-behaved. We are all happy she's here. Veton remarks, "You know, Teacher, in the years when the Serbs were here, Silvete would not feel she could be safe walking with her family in the streets. Serb police were everywhere. They had guns, and there were many, five or six, on every street corner. They would stop us in the streets and ask for our I.D., ask where we were going, ask if we had money and sometimes take it. If you were a young man, like me, they would ask if we were KLA, if we were terrorist. They take us to jail sometimes, and beat us. We were afraid to be on the streets, to go see our friends, to go to school."

Somehow this little girl's presence today has become a symbol of the freedom these Albanian students now enjoy. I'm glad Silvete felt she could bring her to class, and I find myself wishing *all* the students would bring siblings, nieces, and nephews, so our class-family could grow.

A short visit after class with Leonard and his mother at their apartment. Zerife wants to know if I think Leonard did well on the TOEFL. I don't want to tell her the truth; I just tell her that he has studied very hard and I know he did his best. Just realize, I tell her, that most people prepare much longer than Leonard has been able to do. If he doesn't score well this time, he will next time.

"I worry about him," she says. "I don't know what he can do with his life."

"I worry about him, too," I tell her honestly.

MONDAY, JANUARY 29, 2001
Sofia, Bulgaria

We have driven through Macedonia to Sofia, Bulgaria, for a conference of ABA-CEELI attorneys from all over Central and Eastern Europe. As Ed confers, I play tourist, the mud of Prishtina caked on my boots, soiling my pants legs. I feel like the visiting country cousin.

It's so good to be in what feels like a real city. Our elegant and comfortable hotel, the Sheraton Balkan, the exotic architecture of the Alexander Nevski church, the transcendent sounds of Bulgarian Orthodox choirs. Wide boulevards, art galleries, cosmopolitan restaurants, archaeological museums. A visible history, signs of intellectual life, a culture you can see everywhere you look. No mud, no garbage, no bombed buildings.

And I look back on Kosovo and feel such compassion. There was never much there in the way of a significant material culture, especially after Communist construction projects replaced historic buildings. Not much to attract tourists, anyway, even before the war. But now many of the symbols of their history and culture—the mosques and Orthodox churches and monasteries, their old town centers—have gone up in smoke. The artifacts in Kosovo's few museums—those that weren't destroyed or looted and taken to Serbia—are still packed away in boxes in UNMIK basements. Here in Sofia I can look back and see clearly the extent of the Kosovars' isolation, their poverty, their awful plight.

TUESDAY, JANUARY 30, 2001

I hire a local guide to drive me out of Sophia to the medieval Boyana Church, a UNESCO World Heritage Site, full of amazing frescoes. As we drive, I ask the guide, an attractive young woman named Karina, about Bulgarian views of Albanians. She hesitates. "We feel bad for what happened to them," she says carefully, "but we don't think the war [the NATO bombing of Serbia] was necessary." I tell her about the 860,000 Kosovars driven from their country, of the 10,000 civilian dead, of the 187 bodies found on the hill we live on. "Isn't that sufficient reason for war?" I ask. She gives the slightest of shrugs and says, "Some of your bombs fell—as an accident, I know—in our country. Now we know these bombs have depleted uranium and might contaminate our country. NATO hurt Bulgaria, too."

Karina feels little sympathy for Albanians, and she resents NATO and the U.S. as bullies who are throwing their weight around the Balkans.

Today I read in an article in *Newsweek*: "Anti-U.S. feeling is helping to unite Europe in a common culture." And I think: the love of Americans felt by Kosovo Albanians may be unique in the world. Are we loved, even *liked,* anywhere else?

THURSDAY, FEBRUARY 1, 2001
Prishtina

Back home this morning I am thinking about the isolation, the ignorance of *Americans.* We are, by the world's standards, wealthy, and we have virtually unlimited access to news and books and magazines. We can travel, we can learn. But we are an island, cut off from the rest of the world not so much by geography as by complacency, by a lack of curiosity, by arrogance, perhaps. We are worldly, but we know little of the world.

What did I know before last week of Bulgaria's resentment of the U.S.? What did I know before last year of the struggle for power in Yugoslavia? What do I know now of, say, Zimbabwe or Cambodia or Pakistan?

Kosovars have an excuse for being ignorant of the rest of the world. Americans do not.

Later...
Ed comes home tonight with a harrowing tale. He and Pam drove in her OSCE van to the bleak lead-mining city of Mitrovica to attend a war crimes trial today. It is a city, Ed says, that is "divided by hate and a river." As they drove slowly out of the northern, Serb half of the city, leaving the courthouse, a young man ran up to Ed's

passenger-side window and rapped on it furiously. Ed asked Pam to stop. She did, though she didn't like it much. The guy kept motioning for Ed to roll down his window and kept reaching into his pocket, another worrying sign. Eventually he showed the edge of a badge indicating he was an OSCE employee. As Ed rolled down his window a couple of inches, the guy explained in a panicky voice that he was a Serb. Any Serb found working for the U.N. occupiers is a traitor and will be treated as such. This guy had just been found out. Ed and Pam let him in the car and drove like hell for the bridge and over into the Albanian sector, where OSCE headquarters are located. As a Serb, of course, the young man would be in terrible danger from Albanians in the southern part of the city, but at least Ed and Pam put him down in a "safe zone" controlled by KFOR and the U.N. police. Ed says he's "never seen fear so palpable."

So Ed got a close-up view of the worsening violence in Mitrovica. Some of the internationals who live there are moving back to Prishtina to stay until it blows over—if it does. We've offered our spare bedroom to some of the "refugees."

FRIDAY, FEBRUARY 2, 2001

Luan arrives in class looking gloomy. He hasn't been able to get a visa, so he can't go to Freiburg for the engineering course after all. The documents will take several more weeks he says—by then it will be too late.

Visas are, I've learned, another major obstacle here. Even if there is money to leave the country, obtaining a visa to almost any country is very, very difficult. In the first place, when Serbs pushed Albanians out of the country, they seized all their identity papers so there would be less chance they could return. Many Albanians still have not been able to replace passports—or even to prove that they are Kosovars or own their homes, for that matter, for birth records and records of home ownership were also destroyed.

Luan obtained a new passport from UNMIK, but couldn't manipulate the German visa bureaucracy quickly enough.

There will be other courses, he says, trying to smile. "I will keep trying."

SATURDAY, FEBRUARY 3, 2001

Tonight Ed talks about the trial in Mitrovica he's been observing. It's a war crimes trial of a young Serb who is accused of having taken part in the massacre of Albanian men in Mitrovica in the spring of 1999. There is no doubt the men were massacred. Witnesses tell of masked Serbs forcing Albanian families out of their homes, separating the men and boys from the women, children, and old men, whom they put on buses and drove to the border. The bodies of seventeen of the men were later recovered in a mass grave within sight of the town; most had been shot, several had been stabbed. The witness on the stand today is a widow who had lost not only her husband but her father-in-law and other relatives in the massacre. She claims to identify the accused, who was her neighbor, by a limp and a peculiar way of pronouncing a word.

Certainly many Serbs are guilty of this horrible crime. But is *this* Serb guilty? The evidence against the defendant, Ed says, is so flimsy he should never have been indicted. Can the trials of Serbs accused of war crimes be left to Albanian judges who, understandably, are hardly dispassionate in these matters, and who feel pressure from their Albanian community to convict? Albanians deserve justice, but they must also dispense justice, even to the enemy. The U.N. must do something about this, Ed says. And it won't be easy.

MONDAY, FEBRUARY 5, 2001

Tonight I hear a long burst of automatic rifle fire down the street and realize I haven't heard much gunfire lately. Or is it just that I never notice it anymore? There was a bomb scare in front of the school today—CIVPOL investigated and found it to be nothing. But Fatmira and Emina, pretty cousins who live together, tell me that a grenade exploded on their floor of their downtown apartment building last night. Emina could not sleep afterward, and looks haggard today.

In the south, a new Albanian guerrilla force is growing in support of Albanians living in the Preshevo Valley on the border with Serbia. New recruits, new ambushes of Serbs every day. Violence is on the increase, it seems clear.

But tonight all this is overshadowed by my worries about my father. In an e-mail today he speaks of having no stamina, no energy. That's not like Daddy. Has something happened? Has his cancer recurred? It's been almost four years since his diagnosis, and I've read that most patients with his type of cancer die within five years. I tell myself if anyone can beat this thing, Daddy can. But I still worry.

TUESDAY, FEBRUARY 6, 2001

Ed comes home tonight looking distraught. He slumps on the sofa and tells me about Ardita, the new legal assistant in his office. She is, Ed says, one of the sweetest people he's ever met. She told him today that her family lived in a village south of Prishtina. Her 104-year-old great-grandmother lived with several sons and daughters and their sons and daughters—most of them over sixty. When Serb paramilitaries came to their house and demanded they leave, most couldn't. The Serbs—many of whom were neighbors—burned the house down around them. Eleven old people, burned alive. Much of Ardita's extended family.

What can we do here, we ask each other, when the suffering has been so great, the hatreds are so deep, the problems so insurmountable? What could we ever do for this poor war-ravaged non-country? For someone like Ardita who has lost her family? For Blerta and Jehona who have witnessed the horrors of war, for my students who spent their young lives being despised, who seem condemned to a life of poverty and isolation?

"We can only do what we have been doing, offering them encouragement and love," Ed says. This is, we decide, why we are here. Not to create a legal system or even to teach English, but simply to love and encourage these young people who are coming into our lives.

WEDNESDAY, FEBRUARY 7, 2001

Faton comes in right after the class started. He is beaming. "Teacher, I am here only to tell you goodbye." His visa has been approved and he is off tomorrow to study material science for six months in Freiburg. The job with NATO didn't come through, but this did.

I give him a hug. Everyone in the class is happy for him, and shakes his hand. But I see Luan wince when Faton gives us his news. Luan has been trying for several months to get a visa so he can study in Freiburg, with no results. He covers it well, though, and embraces Faton and wishes him well.

We promise to e-mail each other, but tonight I already miss Faton.

THURSDAY, FEBRUARY 8, 2001

Fatmira is seventeen years old, tall, willowy, vivacious, and has the whole class in thrall, especially, of course, the young men. Today she brings in photos of herself in deliberately provocative poses— her innocent notion of what *seductive* looks like, outthrust hip, pouty lips, a bit of décolletage. As the guys gather round to look, Fatmira is flippant and cheerfully disdainful. "I am beautiful, Teacher. I know this! All men love me!" She tosses her head, her long brown hair flying, and laughs, refusing to take herself or her admirers seriously.

Fatmira and her cousin Emina are exceptionally bright, beautiful, independent young women who, they tell me, want to control their own lives, not fall under the control of domineering husbands. They always stay after class for conversation, and they grill me about the life of women in the U.S. They want to know "... everything! Tell us everything, dear Teacher!"

Today I tell them how many women in the U.S. struggle to balance career and family. "You have a career, Teacher, and you have a family," Emina says. "Is it hard for you?"

"Well," I tell her, "it's possible because Ed and I share the household chores and, when our boys were young, we shared the child care. He's a much better housekeeper than I am!" I laugh.

They marvel at this. "Here," Fatmira says, "you would not find many men who would do that. Men in Kosova like to be boss, and they do not like to do the work of women."

"It's that way many places in the U.S. too," I tell them. "These things take time. Kosova can change."

The young women look doubtful, but, as always, kiss me cheerfully as they leave.

FRIDAY, FEBRUARY 9, 2001

After class the Professor, looking distinguished as always in his tweeds, asks me if I could get a medicine, unavailable here, that their doctor prescribed for his wife. He has written down the name: Zoloft. It is, I know, an antidepressant, but I say nothing except to apologize and tell him I have no access to prescription medicines here.

"Ah, it is no matter, Mrs. Paula," he says in his friendly-formal manner. "I will look for some other way." After a pause, "My wife has some psych . . ." (we settle on "psychological") "troubles. She will not get up from her bed." He and his sons bring her food, take care of the house and clothes—everything. The Professor acts unconcerned. But I know he adores his wife, and is very worried.

SATURDAY, FEBRUARY 10, 2001

Today I meet several students at the school and we walk up Dragodan for another meeting of the Hemingway Book Club of Kosova. We have finished reading *The Old Man and the Sea,* and now we will watch the film I brought back from the U.S. I've jerry-rigged a spare cord to the TV, and have arranged with Isa to fire up the generator if the electricity goes out. The generator is small, but should power the TV and our new VCR. (This place is awash in TVs and VCRs—though with little electricity and only scratchy, blurred bootleg movies to watch.)

We sit downstairs and enjoy Cokes and juice while I tell them about the many years Hemingway lived in Cuba, fishing in the Gulf Stream and writing novels and short stories. "You know," I tell them, "when Hemingway wrote *The Old Man and the Sea* he was at a very low point in his life." I explain that he had witnessed the horrors of World War II, during which his son, Jack, had been captured and held as a prisoner of war by the Germans. He was suffering from alcoholism and depression, and the only novel he had written in ten years was a critical disaster. The world thought he was finished as a writer.

But then, he wrote *The Old Man and the Sea,* and he knew he had written the best thing of his life. It was the book, he told friends, that summarized all he had learned about life and about writing. And it was a huge commercial success. When it was first published in *Life* magazine, that issue sold over five million copies.

"Then, the best thing!" I tell the students. He won two of the world's top prizes, the Pulitzer Prize in America, and the Nobel Prize for literature in 1954. The whole world fell in love with *The Old Man and the Sea.*

Not long after the book was published, it was made into a film—the film we're about to see—and it starred one of America's most famous actors, Spencer Tracy, as the old man. But I warn them that in the film Spencer Tracy's voice-over is hard to follow. He speaks very fast. I ask the students to listen for the "gist" of the story. Don't worry about the details.

So we settle down on the sofas and the floor to watch. We watch as Manolin sees the old man off. We follow the old man's effort to catch the marlin, and his long struggle as the marlin pulls him out to sea. We see his cramped, bloody hands, his exhausted, sleep-deprived body. We cheer when the great fish leaps from the water and the old man sees for the first time what he has caught. We hear his love and admiration for the fish: "You are killing me, fish. But you have a right to. Never have I seen a greater, or a calmer or more noble thing than you, brother. Come on and kill me. I do not care who kills who."

And, of course, we watch in horror as the sharks begin to attack his catch. We watch the old man's hopeless fight as he stabs and clubs the sharks, and we sigh when he realizes at last, when the great fish's carcass has been eaten away completely, that he is "beaten now finally and without remedy."

We are comforted by the tender welcome given the old man by the boy when he returns home and, finally, we are thrilled to see that the old man will return to the sea, will try again.

The English has sometimes been hard to follow, but these scenes have needed no translation.

"How did the old man make it through this struggle?" I ask.

"He was strong," says Granit 1.

"But even a strong man can give up. And Santiago was an *old* man!"

"He was strong, yes," says Granit 2, " but he needed more. He had to have courage. He had to reach down into his heart and find courage so he could keep going. And he had to do this over and over."

"So he had courage and he had endurance," I say. "These are the things Hemingway valued most. It is why the old man was a hero to Hemingway, even though he did not bring the fish in."

"What does Hemingway mean when he has the old man say, 'A man can be destroyed but not defeated'?"

They all seem to have a sense of this. "It is what happened to us when the Serbs took away our liberty, made prisoners of us. They killed us, but our hearts remained strong."

"We endured," Granit 2 says.

Hearing this, I remember another passage from the book. "Do you remember how the old man loved turtles?" I ask them, and read the passage, " 'Most people are heartless about turtles because a turtle's heart will beat for hours after he has been cut up and butchered. But the old man thought, I have such a heart, too.'"

They nod their heads and smile.

"What did the old man lose, and what did he win?" I ask.

He lost the fish, we all agree. But he won self-respect and the renewed respect of the villagers. He maintained his dignity and showed courage in the face of overwhelming adversity. And we all know that the love and devotion of the boy, his young friend and apprentice, will be unending.

This film is not a thriller. It is not the kind of action picture young people are used to seeing these days. I can imagine that many American kids would find it dated and boring. But today no one has moved during the entire movie. As we discuss it I can see that many of these students have been greatly moved. They understand, as many students in my own country could not possibly understand, just what Hemingway is talking about.

Emina says, "I will remember this old man, Teacher. I will think of him when things get hard."

And Granit 2 nods in his serious way. He has been particularly taken with this story. I hope, in all the hard times to come in Granit's life—in the lives of all these students—they will think of the old man and take courage.

Tonight I know that, in the hard times to come in *my* life, I will think of my *students* and take courage. I am their teacher, but today, as always, it is my students who teach me.

SUNDAY, FEBRUARY 11, 2001

A sad day. Kate leaves today to go back to the U.S. She has become a dear, dear friend for both Ed and me, and Ed has loved working with her every day. His office, our lives here, won't be the same without her gentle, quiet manner, her intelligence and good humor.

Three weeks ago she developed a bad toothache and went to a dentist recommended by one of the local ABA-CEELI staff. He wrenched the tooth from her jaw and sent her off with no pain-killers and no antibiotics. She developed awful pain in her jaw, couldn't open it after a while, and soon had fever and was very sick. We gave her some of our medicine for pain, and a doctor at the U.S. Mission unofficially told her which antibiotic she should buy. (He's not really supposed to treat people other than Mission staff.) But things have not gotten much better. She needs the care of a specialist. It has all been too much for our dear friend.

And now she is leaving, for good, and we feel like there's been a death in the family. Tonight she gives me a turquoise and silver pin to remember her by. I know I will always remember Kate.

Monday, February 12, 2001

As the snow melts, the filth and stench of the city are worse than ever. The streets have turned to mud, as slick and slippery as ice. As I walk down Dragodan today I almost fall several times. A fall today wouldn't be as funny as the fall in the snow. On the sidewalks I kick garbage out of the way to create a path. By the stadium the black marketeers have placed their socks and knives, cigarettes and white lace curtains on tarps that seem to float on the mud. And on the bombed-out Serb police building next to the stadium, some clever entrepreneur has hung his Persian-style rugs from the gutted third and fourth floors.

Today before class I meet with Granit 1. He came after class last week to ask if I could help him with two things: (1) He wants to go to America to study in high school and (2) he wants to be a detective, like my son Paul. Today I give him information on two programs that help international students spend a year at an American high school. And I have set up an appointment for him to meet with an American who works for the UNMIK police. Charley will give Granit good advice about how to further his career aims.

As always, though, money will be the issue. Can Granit's family afford the $10,000 it will take for him to spend a year abroad? Clearly, no. Granit could hardly afford to replace the textbook he dropped in the "muddy water."

I feel so depressed tonight. Sometimes it seems that all I can provide these students is information about impossibilities. I must begin to do something to make things *possible*.

TUESDAY, FEBRUARY 13, 2001

It seems there's a new restaurant or boutique in every block of the city, and it's here, in these new struggling enterprises, that you can see how hard Prishtinans are trying to be "Western." So much work has gone into each café—the linen tablecloths and napkins, the stuccoed walls often painted in desert southwest colors with posters from Santa Fe or California or Tuscany, the meticulously dressed waiters who wish you a cheery *"Bon appétit!"* on serving your meal. But the food itself—unlike their traditional Albanian fare, which is delicious—is often a tasteless imitation of other cuisines. And the menus in English translation provide unintended entertainment. Tonight I tried to order the "chicken buttocks on screwers," but they were out. Must be a popular dish.

I am always so touched—and impressed—by these efforts to leap over generations of neglect and abuse, of Communism and apartheid, and to establish efficient, modern enterprises. Surely these shops and restaurants survive only as a result of the false economy—a tourist economy, essentially—the international community brings. What will happen when all of us "tourists" leave?

Wednesday, February 14, 2001

I am sitting on the floor of Ed's office working on his financial reports when Jehona comes in, and as always, sweeps me up in a bear hug. Blerta is right behind her and adds her hug as well. "Paula!" Jehona exclaims. "Why do you always sit on the floor to do your work? Why do you not take a desk?" Blerta adds, "You do not care to look dignified?"

"No," I laugh. "I'm comfortable on the floor, and I can spread all my work out and get everything done efficiently this way. I don't much care if I look dignified or not."

"I like this," Blerta comments. "This is very American, I think."

Later I go down to the school and before class talk awhile with Abdul, one of the local English teachers. I compliment him on his English, and he tells me he lived in England for two years. "Unfortunately," he says, "I was in England when war broke out here. After the Serbs starting killing our people and driving them from their homes, I contacted leaders of the KLA, and asked if I could come join them. They told me no. I was the only son, they said. They did not want only sons to join the fighting unless things got so bad they had no choice. They told me to stay in England." Abdul's face is tormented as he tells me this, as he remembers. "This will live with me until my dying day," he says, "this awful truth that I did not get to fight for my fatherland."

"But you are doing good things for your country now," I tell him. "With the English Kosovars learn from you, they can have better lives, have a chance for a future."

"But I did not get to *fight!*" He shakes his head, unconvinced by my feeble consolations.

THURSDAY, FEBRUARY 15, 2001

After class, Leonard seems shaken. He forgot to bring his tuition money today, and the school manager threatened to make him go home. He talked the manager out of it, but his brusque manner has upset him, made him "nervous" as he puts it.

I realize more and more that Leonard, like many of his countrymen, is full of hidden anxieties. The sensitivity, the sweetness that make him so perceptive and caring also leave him vulnerable. And he lived so long in a threatening and corrupt society that he trusts no one in power—except Americans. He is an unhappy combination of innocence and cynicism, and I'm afraid he will suffer because of it.

FRIDAY, FEBRUARY 16, 2001

At the bottom of Dragodan at an intersection close to the railway tracks, there's a sign that proudly proclaims: "This Corner Cleaned Up by UNMIK." The signpost itself is invisible because of the mountains of rubbish piled around it. The trash of kitchens, offices, and shops surrounds the sign and spills over into the street.

There's a basic cultural misunderstanding on this corner. UNMIK, wishing to set an example for the community, cleaned up the site and erected the sign to show what could be done. The community took the sign to mean that UNMIK would clean up whatever garbage they dumped there. Thus, the messiest corner in the city.

SATURDAY, FEBRUARY 17, 2001

The internationals here seem to be a melancholy lot. They are mostly single, or have left families at home and so are often lonely, sad, depressed. And there is a lot of illness—upper respiratory infections, intestinal disorders. Many are frustrated by language and cultural barriers, by the Kosovars' fierce individualism—in everything from trash collection to law codification—an individualism bordering on anarchy. Pam tells me many internationals don't like the Kosovo Albanians. They consider them to be sneaky, stubborn, lazy, uncooperative, dishonest. (Time for an international class on stereotypes.) But I don't see many internationals spending time with local people, not socially, anyway. They escape for long weekends in Greece or Vienna whenever they can, and they seek each others' company in restaurants almost every night.

Ed and I survive so well, I think, because we have made Albanian friends, and especially because we have each other. After twenty-two years we still enjoy each other's company. We look forward to sharing stories each night, and we know the comforting shoulder is always there when one of us begins to feel blue, to miss the familiar touchstones of home.

Tonight, Ed takes my hand and says in a low, teasing voice, "Let me lead you to the seraglio." He walks me upstairs to our favorite room, the "Red Salon." The white lace curtains glow in the light of candles he has placed around the room. He has put my favorite violin concerto on the CD player. We lie down on the long red velvet sofa and are reminded of other reasons we're glad to be here together.

SUNDAY, FEBRUARY 18, 2001

I finish my lesson plan and decide to take a walk. The air is crisp, the street is quiet. I walk to one end of the street where a KFOR gun emplacement appears to guard a pizza restaurant (though it actually guards the rear entrance of the U.S. Mission), and gaze out onto the snow-covered mountains in the far distance. Because the air is so polluted, it was months before I knew the mountains were there. The clearer winter air has revealed them, and I come now almost every day to take a look and a deep breath. I walk in the other direction and suddenly the sky over the street is filled with blackbirds, thousands of them, blocking out what is left of the failing light, their hoarse cries shattering the tranquility of the early evening. As I reach the cemetery at the other end of the street, blackbirds have settled on the tombstones, but after a while these birds are quiet, and the cemetery is hushed. At the entrance to the cemetery a large monument marks the graves of Bajram Kelmendi and his two young sons. Kelmendi's reputation as a skilled human rights lawyer who, during 1998, had provided information to the war crimes tribunal, marked him for death in the early days of the war. He and his sons were taken from their home and murdered by Serb policemen on the night of March 24, 1999. Bouquets of plastic flowers lean against their tombstone this evening; three blackbirds sit silently on its top.

MONDAY, FEBRUARY 19, 2001

In the north a busload of Serbs, families with children, was blown up Friday. The bus obliterated, eleven people dead, including a baby. Dozens were wounded. The families were returning to their homes in Kosovo after a visit to Serbia, and were being escorted by several armed KFOR vehicles for their protection. The bomb, placed in a culvert under the road, was devastatingly precise—no KFOR vehicles harmed, just the bus. The news report today calls it "one of the bloodiest and most brazen attacks on Serb civilians since NATO-led peacekeepers and United Nations administrators took control of the province twenty months ago." Local Albanian newspapers express horror and outrage.

Albanian terrorists are suspected, but today when I arrive in class Leonard is quick to say, "It wasn't us, Teacher. Think about it." He has this all worked out. "It must have been Serbs. It was close to their border, they put the bomb in the bus before it left the country to make it look like it was us, to make it look like we are bad people."

"Leonard, don't you believe there are a *few* Albanians who could have done something like this?"

"Well . . . yes, maybe." But he doesn't believe it, really. Nor, I expect, do most Serbs believe that fellow Serbs could have committed atrocities in Bosnia or Kosovo.

When will they be able to say "a few Serbs" instead of "the Serbs," or "some Albanians" instead of "the Albanians"? Collective guilt, collective innocence. This notion is a central problem in the Balkans.

TUESDAY, FEBRUARY 20, 2001

Luan was not in class today, but as I was leaving he came bounding up the stairs, breathless, to say he had just returned from Macedonia and had been granted his German visa. He'll leave for Germany tomorrow to take a brief course in metals testing. He is elated. Finally!

Tonight I am so happy.

WEDNESDAY, FEBRUARY 21, 2001

Amira is the only non-Albanian in my class. She is a Russian Jew who immigrated to Israel three years ago, and is now in Kosovo with her husband, a U.N. diplomat. She asked me early on not to mention she is from Russia—Russians are traditional allies of the Serbs—but to say only that she is Israeli. Although her English is shaky, she speaks five other languages fluently. She speaks with a quiet voice, and her eyes are full of kindness.

Today she tells me that yesterday, as she and her husband were returning from Skopje, their car was stopped by a gang of angry Serbs wielding clubs and sticks. The Serbs demanded to know if there were any Albanians in the car. Fortunately, somehow antici-pating trouble, Amira and her husband had left their Albanian friend at the border. Otherwise . . .

Since last week's bus-bombing, many Serbs have been going wild, demonstrating, throwing stones, burning cars, beating people up. The victims are mostly Albanians, but some internationals have been targeted, too. We've been warned not to travel within the country, to be especially careful.

Ed was supposed to travel to Mitrovica again this week, taking three young Albanian lawyers with him. Alma, Ardita, and Ahmet all wanted to make the trip, but Ed called it off. Mitrovica is proba-bly the most dangerous town in Europe right now. What would he do, he asked me, if their car were stopped and these young Albani-ans were attacked? How could he protect them?

THURSDAY, FEBRUARY 22, 2001

Emina's beautiful eyes usually look haunted. Although she is naturally vivacious and cheerful, I can see that she struggles against despair. She has not talked to me of her own life during the apartheid. But she tells me today that life for Albanian women under Milosevic's regime was a horror. "Women were picked up off the streets by police," she says, "and were taken to jails and raped. Sometimes they did not come out of the jails. We were afraid to go on the streets."

Today she has brought me a newspaper article. "Rape is a crime Kosovars do not usually talk about, Teacher. It is considered shameful. But this newspaper, it recently had articles about rapes during the war. They are talking about how rape was used to terrify Albanians, to drive us from the country. So maybe there is some change now and women will have some justice." But her eyes tell me she doesn't really believe in such justice.

FRIDAY, FEBRUARY 23, 2001

The Professor, Leonard, Leutrim, and Drita stay after class today to write on the white board. Leutrim always loves to work at the board, to demonstrate the English skills he learned as a refugee in New Jersey. He writes sentences, underlining past perfect verbs with a flourish, turning with a grin to receive my praise.

I then ask the Professor if he will tell us something about Richard Feynman's theories about subatomic particles. In English. I know he admires Feynman, and last week gave him a copy of Feynman's *The Meaning of It All*.

"Ah, Mrs. Paula. This is a very difficult thing you ask me!" But he approaches the white board with relish, drawing a diagram, explaining in his broken English these ideas that excite him so much, searching our eyes to make sure we are following him. What a good teacher he is! His students must love him.

SATURDAY, FEBRUARY 24, 2001

Today I pick up Tim Judah's *Kosovo: War and Revenge* again for the sole purpose of reminding myself of the awfulness of what happened here. I read again of the massacres, the rapes, the brutal ethnic cleansing.

It is so easy to forget that there was war, apartheid, terror here. I am anesthetized by the people themselves. They stroll the streets and meet friends in cafés for coffee and sweets; Dragodan vibrates with new construction activity. Igballe and Isa seem so happy, so . . . normal. But as I look up from my laptop now I see the white walls of this pleasant salon and think of the masked paramilitaries who drove Igballe, Isa, and Agim from their home, who killed a feral cat and flung its blood on these very walls, now so clean and white. Of the neighbor up the street who was shot because he didn't get out fast enough.

Judah's book, these walls, help me remember what lies beneath the surface.

SUNDAY, FEBRUARY 25, 2001

The electricity is off about half the time now, the water about half the time. What we hope for is the happy coincidence that gives us hot water for a bath—though that hasn't occurred in the last four days. Igballe and Isa installed a small wood stove in the kitchen—

today I fire it up to take the edge off the cold downstairs. As with most things here, it's a trade-off. Warmth and smoke, or frigid, but clear air. Today I opt for warmth and smoke.

It is Ed's sixtieth birthday. Jehona and Blerta, his legal assistants, and Ardiana, a friend of theirs who works with OSCE, come tonight for a celebration. I have made stewed chicken with tomatoes and onions, and Jehona and Blerta, our "adopted daughters" have brought him an iced cake: "Happy Birthday Our Big Daddy." They adore him. As do I.

I ask Blerta, a native of Albania, about her work in the refugee camps. Moved by the plight of the hundreds of thousands of Kosovars streaming across the border into her country with only the clothes on their backs, Blerta had left home to assist doctors in the camps. "It was terrible," she says. "Women who were so worried about their missing husbands that they could not cook or clean or care for their children. Old couples moaning that it was *they* who should be dead, not their sons, their daughters, their grandchildren. Young children who had seen so much they were not normal any longer." Blerta is an intense young woman who yearns to study international and human rights law. Observing her these last few months I have wondered where she gets her fierce drive and ambition. As she tells me these stories I begin to understand.

She used to visit a sixteen-year-old girl who lived in a tent with her mother and sister. "In the morning of that terrible day when the Serbs came to their village," Blerta tells us, "the mother, the son, and the daughters knelt in a circle to pray that God would stop the terrible things that were happening. The father had left for the mountains to join the fighters. They were still on the ground in the circle when the soldiers crashed in." The soldiers grabbed the son and took him outside. The family continued to pray until they heard a shot. "They were shocked and remained still," Blerta says, recounting the girl's story. "They could not cry, and were not able even to scream."

The soldiers came back into the house, grabbed the mother and, in front of her daughters, raped her. Each soldier raped the mother as the girls cried and screamed. When they were finished, the soldiers told them all to leave their house, to leave the country. The girls picked up their mother, supporting her under each arm, and began walking. "They were thinking it was just a bad dream and they had to go away in order to wake up." They walked for days without talking, finally joining other people who had just lived through their own hells and were moving toward the border camps.

The girl told her, Blerta said, that she still keeps hoping she will wake up to find that it was all just a bad dream. But her brother is gone and her mother has not spoken a word since that day. She is beginning to realize that it is all true, that she will not wake up, and that these memories will torment her forever.

"Her story made me realize," Blerta says, "how violent the world can be. It changed everything for me."

Ed then tells us a story he heard today from an NBC stringer during the war who usually has the facts. During the war, just outside Prizren, a Serb, overwhelmed by the brutality of his own army, placed himself in front of a column of tanks on their way to destroy another Albanian village. A scene, Ed says, from Tienanmen Square. Except that this time the world wasn't watching and the tanks didn't stop. The Serb soldier was ground under the treads of the tanks, a martyr to decency.

It is the first such story we have heard, and Ardiana, a bright Kosovo Albanian college graduate who hangs out with Blerta and Jehona, isn't happy with it. "Why do you tell stories like this?" she cries. "I don't want to hear about one good Serb!" Ardiana is a thoughtful, kindhearted young woman, but some part of her fears that to believe in one good Serb might be to believe in other good Serbs, a concept that belies her own experience.

Ardiana, whose family suffered greatly in the war, is trying to come to terms with the evil she has seen up close. She struggles against the certainty of evil, but, as with the story of the courageous Serb, also against the possibility of good.

MONDAY, FEBRUARY 26, 2001

Today I must tell Igballe about the ants and find out where to get ant killer. Tricky, because I don't want to accuse her of renting us a house with *ants!* Nor do I want her to buy us anything. I just want her to tell me where to buy some ant killer.

So, I knock on her door, ask her to come around to our part of the house, and show her my hand-drawn picture of an ant. Then I point to the place I think they are getting in, and walk my fingers on the floor to demonstrate. Igballe still looks puzzled; I'm not the artist I'd like to be. So I pull out the Albanian-English, English-Albanian dictionary, which I use *only* as a last resort because Igballe and I have to share my reading glasses—back and forth, back and forth. She puts on my glasses.

"Ah, *mize!*"

Now, she must look up something to show me. This is where it gets painful because, although Igballe is a primary school teacher, she has not yet mastered alphabetical order. Her word search is done almost at random. After a long time she points to a word and I see the English: Chalk. *"Chalk?"*

Igballe leaves and comes back in a few minutes with a small packet from which she takes a piece of, yes, chalk. She then draws three small squares, about four inches per side, on the wooden floor by the ant highway. I follow her from room to room, as she carefully draws three more squares in each room.

A couple of hours later I check. And sure enough, in the vicinity of each square lie scores of dead ants. Furthermore, nowhere in the house—once teaming with hundreds of ants—can I find a single live one.

A Balkan hex? Is it the chalk, or the shape? Or a lethal combination? Whatever it is, I doubt it would pass EPA regulations. What is this stuff? As with most things here, it doesn't pay to inquire too closely.

TUESDAY, FEBRUARY 27, 2001

Emina, she of the statuesque figure and the Liz Taylor eyes, has a job. A real job with OSCE, making real money. She had interviewed with many organizations, and, in her usual independent, self-confident way, had turned down some positions, preferring to wait for just the right opportunity. Good for Emina! I announce her success to the class and everyone applauds, happy to see one of their group get a break.

Tonight I write this journal entry on my laptop. Other nights I have handwritten the entries in notebooks. Sometimes I jot down notes as I ride home in the cab or wait for an appointment. I want all of this—everything and everyone—to stay with me.

WEDNESDAY, FEBRUARY 28, 2001

The taxi driver tells me today, "We love Americans too much." His grammar mistake accidentally hits upon the truth: It may not be long before we Americans start to disappoint Kosovars, and they will think their affections, their trust, were misplaced. We are pampering Serbia's Kostunica, we are delaying national elections in Kosovo, and many Americans who worked in Kosovo are leaving the country—some for posts in newly opened offices in Belgrade. And does our government have the will to stick around long enough to help them build a nation? We are already beginning to cut funding for American positions here.

How much longer will we be loved?

THURSDAY, MARCH 1, 2001

As Leonard and I walk from the Monaco Café to the school today, I ask him: "Leonard, how is it that people here can always tell I am an American? Even before I open my mouth, shopkeepers, taxi drivers, people on the street can see that I am from the U.S." I've been puzzled about this for a long while.

"That is easy, Teacher," he says. "You are not afraid."

I don't understand.

"Teacher"—he eyes me carefully, not wanting to insult me—"you think that because you like everyone, everyone will like you. You show everyone a friendly face, a face that trusts. You don't think anyone would hurt you. Everyone knows that is how Americans are."

"Here in Kosova," he continues, "we have learned to be afraid. Americans have not learned this lesson."

FRIDAY, MARCH 2, 2001

Now that we've finished *The Old Man and the Sea,* the Hemingway Book Club of Kosova continues in discussions after class and on days between classes. The Cambridge School has kindly given me permission to have as many meetings of the club as we want, as long as we can find classrooms not in use. We continue to weave the class in with the club.

Now we're reading short stories I brought with me from the U.S. and have copied for everyone: Poe's "The Tell-Tale Heart," Ambrose Bierce's "An Occurrence at Owl Creek Bridge," and, the Professor's favorite, O. Henry's "Gift of the Magi." "This is *love!*" he says. With these stories we explore some of the great themes of American literature, and, of course, we are entertained by some of the best plots. These students love a good plot!

But it is Kate Chopin's "The Story of an Hour" that I've been especially eager for them to read. The story: In the course of only an hour a young wife hears her husband has been killed in a train wreck, mourns for him, then begins to feel relieved, liberated, happy, and finally, when her husband walks in the door, having missed the train, she falls dead of the shock. People think she died of happiness.

This nineteenth-century feminist story about repressed wives being introduced to young people in Kosovo? Yes. They are ready for it, and they need it. Emina tells me today: "Teacher, the woman in this story knows her husband is a good man, and that he loves her. But she has no freedom. Her marriage is a prison."

Women have come a long way since the nineteenth century, I tell her.

"Not in Kosova," she says. "Here, things are still the same. If you marry, your husband can tell you what to do. You have to ask him if you can go visit your mother for the afternoon. You are his prisoner."

This is what I have heard. The ancient Kanun of Lek states that a "woman is a superfluity in the household." As to a girl's rights in marriage, the Kanun says if she "does not submit and marry her fiancé, she should be handed over to him by her parents by force, to-gether with a cartridge, and if the girl tries to flee, her husband may kill her with her parents' cartridge." The Kanun has been officially outlawed, and urban Kosovars might laugh at it today. But some of its precepts seem to have become deeply embedded in the culture.

The boys have not particularly taken to Chopin's tale. Seeing that it's a "woman's story," some have not bothered to read it. They are more interested in the suspense of "The Tell-Tale Heart" and the drama of "An Occurrence at Owl Creek Bridge." But Kate Chopin's heroine touched the hearts of the young women in the class. I hope Fatmira, Emina, Edona, Drita, Fazile, Silvete, Dafina, Blerta, Jehona, Nora, all these young women I have come to love so much, will choose mates who respect them, treat them as equal partners. Emina, clearly, fears it won't happen like that.

SATURDAY, MARCH 3, 2001

I can hardly believe it, but it looks as though we will have to go back to the U.S. by the end of April. Ed's projects for ABA-CEELI will be coming to an end in a few weeks, and the positions he's been of-fered by the U.N. and OSCE—interesting, important judicial work that could keep us here—require U.S. funding for Americans. Our government has frozen funding for these jobs in Kosovo indefi-nitely. Like some European countries, the U.S. is beginning to pull back from Kosovo, losing interest, and Ed and I are caught in the middle of it.

At home, our tenant has become ill and is canceling her lease. And my father . . . I am beginning to suspect all is not well with him.

Events here and at home are conspiring against us. We will leave at the end of April. We are heartbroken.

SUNDAY, MARCH 4, 2001

A startling thing tonight. I look at my journal entry of a year ago. It was one of the few days last year that I bothered to write anything down. Here's what I wrote, March 4, 2000:

> This week, on the seventh of March, will be the thirty-fifth anniversary of the Pettus Bridge march in Selma, Alabama. I watched old news footage on television tonight. I was a young college student at the time and I am sure that I was either oblivious of the march and its historic importance, or I was angry about it. I had brought to college the ignorant, racist views of my southern heritage. I was so wrong, so blind, and today I am so ashamed of that young woman who was me.

Even knowing that I was just a product of my culture and time—a small, poor southern town in the 1950s—does little, even tonight, to mitigate my feelings of remorse and regret. In those days I didn't even notice that the black teenagers in my hometown were being bussed sixty miles to high school because they weren't allowed to go to our "white" schools. Nor did I care that black people weren't allowed in "our" restaurants, and were made to use segregated toilets and water fountains. But as I read last year's journal entry I think about where I am today. In Prishtina, Kosovo, teaching students who have suffered discrimination all their lives. Although I know I can never be color-blind, I would like to believe that I am a different person from that nineteen-year-old who was so full of ignorance and prejudice. My hometown in Arkansas, too, our entire nation has undergone a sea change since the days of the march in Selma.

Mulling this over tonight I know that it was my liberal education that opened my eyes. In college and graduate school, as I began to study history, the myths that had fed my ignorance were shattered; as I learned about different cultures and societies, the stereotypes that had fostered my prejudice began to dissolve. Education was the antidote for the poison in my heart.

Of course, as I write this I realize education per se isn't the answer. I think of the many highly educated members of the Nazi party in Germany, and of Radovan Karadzic, the psychiatrist-poet who led the Bosnian Serbs and who is now indicted for atrocious war crimes. Karadzic is a highly educated monster. Books, schools can teach people to hate as well as to love, to exclude as well as to embrace.

No, there is no one solution for hatred and racism. There may not be any solutions at all. But a liberal education in which students are encouraged to look beyond their own cultural boundaries, and are taught to explore a wide range of ideas, is at least a place to start.

MONDAY, MARCH 5, 2001

More fighting broke out yesterday in Macedonia between Albanian separatists and Macedonian Slavs. Kosovo Albanian fighters are slipping across the border to join the rebels. Macedonia has closed the border and Blerta, among many others, is stuck in Skopje, unable to get back to Kosovo. Because most air travel is done in and out of Skopje, this border closing makes me feel claustrophobic, trapped.

In class, we talk about Kostunica, the new president of Yugoslavia, about his failure to turn Milosevic over to the U.N. War Crimes Tribunal at The Hague. The young students are furious at this, but the Professor says he understands Kostunica's problem. Although the Professor wants Milosevic tried and sentenced as much as anyone, he can see that Kostunica cannot casually hand over the former president. The Professor's is always a thoughtful view. I wonder again about his personal experience in the war; how is he able to remain so philosophical? Did he escape the traumas experienced by most of his countrymen?

The subject turns to forgiveness. Is it possible to forgive? The class consensus is that it might be, someday, but that it is too soon. And besides, they say, no one in Serbia has asked for forgiveness. No one, including Kostunica, has expressed the slightest remorse for anything done in Bosnia, Croatia, or here in Kosovo. Kostunica has merely expressed his opinion that wrongs were done on all sides. That is not enough.

The Professor's view is that the willingness to forgive is the noblest of human impulses. The younger students are respectful of his opinion, but most, clearly, think he is a dreamer.

And what of justice? I ask. What would it take for you to feel you have justice? Would it be enough if Milosevic were tried and sentenced? If Serbia acknowledged its crimes and made a formal apology?

No! Various students tell me in their different ways. This would not be justice! Milosevic was only the leader of the many thousands of Serbs who killed us. And no apology would be sincere because Serbs are big liars! The consensus is this: We just want Serbia to release our prisoners and then leave us alone forever! We never want to have to deal with them again. Just leave us alone!

I frankly have no idea how to guide this discussion. Not for the first time, I look at the faces of these young people and wonder, Is their bitterness, their fear so great that they could do to Serbs what Serbs did to them? Could soft-spoken Veton burn a Serb village because his own was burned by Serbs? Would sweet, wide-eyed Enver, who loves basketball and never misses a class, stand by and watch while atrocities were committed? Could any of these bright, kindhearted young people *kill* Serbs because they are Serbs?

And if I were in their shoes, what would I be capable of? Have I come to grips with the darkness in my own heart?

Tonight I read the words of François Bizot, who was imprisoned by the Khmer Rouge for three months in 1971 and who writes in *Le Portail*: "Every war needs killers and they can always be found. We always put ourselves in the skin of the victims and not of their killers—we never put ourselves in the skin of a Nazi or Khmer Rouge. Yet between them and us there is very little difference, no more than between the victim and us."

And the same from Matthew Spender: "In extreme situations only chance divides the role of the torturer from that of his victims."

Are they right? Given the right circumstances, are we all, even the best of us, capable of anything? There are no easy answers, in Kosovo or anywhere else.

TUESDAY, MARCH 6, 2001

Ed and I get in the Jeep and drive toward Peja. On a recent trip there, he had spotted a devastated, deserted village off the highway he now wants to see up close. We hear that the roads in this direction are safe right now—no one throwing stones, no land mines, no roadblocks.

Just when he's beginning to think it had been a figment of his imagination, he sees it down in a valley. We find the road, and descend into a nightmare landscape. Here is a ghost village that before the war, Ed has learned, was occupied by both Serbs and Albanians. But the town was blown and battered to bits, first by Serbs who destroyed Albanian houses with tanks, artillery, and grenades, and later by returning Albanians who, in their fury, took hammers and brickbats to Serb houses. The whole town destroyed brick by brick, house by house, with a deliberate calculation that left everyone homeless. Bright yellow tape now marks sites of unexploded shells or land mines.

This is one of hundreds of villages wiped off the map by hate. It occurs to me as we look around how the word "village," like the word "peasant," distances us. In my life, as I've heard news reports about the destruction of "villages," whether in Vietnam, Bosnia, or Kosovo, I've sometimes pictured places quaint or primitive or mythical, the storybook homes of Hansel and Gretel, maybe, of people so unlike myself that they would not mourn their dead. Yet, here, today, a rusted cook stove lies on its back in a muddy yard. A solitary blue wall stands amid a pile of rubble, all that remains of some family's cheerful parlor. A real place where real people lived, and died, and, yes, mourned. This village is no fairy tale.

As we drive out of town we pass two KFOR tanks and two armored personnel carriers coming in. The soldiers stare at us. They look at home in this scene of destruction; we, a couple of middle-aged Americans in a white SUV, do not.

WEDNESDAY, MARCH 7, 2001

Walking to work today I see throngs of young men on street corners holding the Albanian flag, the black double-headed eagle on a blood-red field—surely the most aggressive flag I've ever seen. They are being watched carefully by CIVPOL. Carloads of young men waving flags out the windows offer visible support for the Macedonian Albanian "liberation" army.

I ask my students today what they think of the rebels in Macedonia. Genti quickly protests: "They are not rebels, Teacher! You must not call them rebels!"

"But they are rebels, Genti," I say. And the Professor calms him: "Rebel is not a bad word, Genti. It does not mean terrorist."

I see the problem now. "No, Genti. In America we rebelled against the British. A rebel is simply someone who fights against those in power."

"Oh." Genti is embarrassed and apologetic. "I am sorry, Teacher. I was wrong."

I ask again what they think of the fighting in Macedonia. Most approve. The Albanian minority there are oppressed, have no rights, says Leonard. The Professor elaborates: They are not allowed to go to good schools, they have no Albanian-language university, they are not permitted good government jobs. They cannot improve themselves socially and economically.

But what about the violence, I ask? There are many ways to fight injustice. Is violence the only way to solve the problem in Macedonia?

Surprisingly, it is Drita, in her shy, quiet voice, who answers. "No one knew who *we* were, Teacher, until we started fighting. We tried peaceful means for years. The world had never heard of Kosova, of Kosova Albanians until we took up our guns. We tried everything else."

She is right. Despite their tradition as fierce fighters, Kosovo Albanians engaged in peaceful resistance for years, sure that the West would notice their plight, admire their nonviolent struggle, and come to their aid. But Europe and the U.S. gave their efforts only cursory recognition, and in the 1995 Dayton Peace Accords that ended the slaughter in Bosnia, Kosovo was ignored altogether. Not until the KLA started killing the oppressive Serb police and security forces after 1995 did the world focus its attention on Kosovo.

And the world would probably never have known about the injustices done the Macedonian Albanians unless they had taken up *their* guns. One of the troubling lessons of the Balkans seems to be that violence *does* sometimes pay. Still . . . (There is a "still," isn't there?)

As I write this I hear the deep *Whump! Whump! Whump!* of helicopter gunships overhead, that terrible sound we remember from Vietnam war news coverage.

THURSDAY, MARCH 8, 2001

The streets are full of flowers. Men, women, and children with bouquets of flowers in their hands. In the travel agency where I go on business I discover it is "Women's Day." Grown women everywhere are presented with gifts and flowers, and, presumably, are treated with special care on their day. Drita has brought me flowers. Later today Emina, who couldn't attend class, calls me to wish me well, and my landlady, Igballe, knocks on the door bearing a beautifully wrapped bottle of perfume. I am embarrassed that I knew nothing of this holiday and have nothing to give my friends in return.

There are some wry jokes floating around among the flowers, though. "Why is today Women's Day?" the most common joke goes. "Because in Kosovo all other days are for the men."

More fighting on the Macedonian border. The border is closed again. It heads the news tonight on the BBC.

FRIDAY, MARCH 9, 2001

Today, after the break, I sit with the students at our long table and tell them I have news that makes me very, very sad. My husband's work has changed, and some problems have come up at home that must be addressed. I will be leaving Kosovo in a few weeks and won't be able to teach them the upper intermediate course after all.

There is a stunned silence. Some of the girls start to cry quietly. Some of the boys, I think, are trying not to. I can't look at Leonard.

I had met him at the Monaco Café before class to tell him privately, to hold his hand and talk awhile with him. "I have to leave you, Leonard," I told him. "But I will never desert you."

I tell them I have grown to love each one of them. Being their teacher has been the most rewarding experience of my life.

And more.

Trying to perk us all up, I remind them that we have more weeks together, and lots more English to learn! But something has been lost.

When class is over I see several students standing around the Professor. "I am telling them, Mrs. Paula," he says, "that they have just seen one of the good and one of the sad things about being a teacher. We love our students, and then we must leave them, or they must leave us." I think again what a good teacher he must be. What a good *man* he must be.

They file somberly out of class, like mourners at a funeral. Leonard and the Professor are the only students who stay behind today for "conversation." I stay at my position at the head of our long table; they sit on either side of me.

I decide to ask the Professor about his wartime experience.

Five Serb policemen came to his house one day in May, he says. When they asked where he was from, he said his home was Prizren. From this, and from the fact that he spoke fluent Turkish to one of the soldiers, they mistook him for a Turk. This probably saved his life. When they searched the house, he showed them his library full of books. He had hidden his English and Albanian books behind books in Russian and Serbian, he tells me with a smile. The police were pleased to see books in those Slavic languages, but they were suspicious because he had so *many* books. He was a high school teacher, he told them. (A colleague who had admitted the week before to being a college professor had had all his fingers broken by his interrogators.) One policeman fumed that young Albanians were being taught to hate the Serbs. The Professor nodded sadly, saying that he was very distressed that people outside the schools were filling the minds of young Albanians with such propaganda, and that he did his best to set the record straight for his own students.

A cool man in a crisis, this Professor.

After a couple of hours of harassment, during which time the Professor's two boys, eighteen and twenty-one, were being held upstairs, the police left, but only after extracting from him the promise that he would register for his green card first thing the next morning. He didn't do that, of course, for the registration would have identified him and his military-aged sons as Albanians, with dire consequences.

His wife, he said, watched quietly as these tense interrogations were going on. They all lived through the next months waiting for another knock at the door.

"You had a narrow escape, Professor," I comment.

"Yes, we were lucky. But my wife . . ."

I know there is more to this story, and that he needs to tell it. The three of us are quiet for a long while.

Finally, "My wife was O.K. for more than a year after that. I thought she was O.K., anyway. But then, in January this year she started to say all the time, 'What if they had taken our sons? What if they had taken you? What if they had killed us all?' And she says these things over and over and over, all day. And then she went to the bed and wouldn't get up, only saying over and over, 'What if, what if?' She is still in bed most of the time."

Post-traumatic stress disorder, I think to myself. The reason for the Zoloft prescription.

I am very, very sorry, Professor, I tell him. I hope she recovers.

"Ah, yes, well, I think she will be better . . . yes." He has seemed very matter-of-fact telling his story, merely a teacher giving his class a history lesson.

Our conversation gradually turns to other things, until finally the Professor says, in his warm, courtly way, "Mrs. Paula, I am very sorry you will be going. And I wish you and your husband the best of everything. We will miss you."

"Leaving here is the hardest thing I've ever had to do," I tell him, trying to keep from bursting into tears.

Leonard tries to comfort me. "We men, we must not cry even when we want to, but it is O.K. for women to cry, Teacher."

And then I look at the Professor and see that he has put his head in his hands, and is sobbing. He pulls a white handkerchief from his pocket, takes his glasses off and wipes his face.

"I am sorry, Mrs. Paula." He can hardly talk. "It is just . . ."

I want to get up and put my arms around him, hold him, but I just put my hand on his arm. "Please don't be sorry, Professor. It is a time to cry." About so many things.

After a long moment, the Professor gets up and paces the floor, tears still streaming. Leonard and I sit quietly. Leonard looks stricken. When he can talk again, the Professor says, "I am not the man I was before the war."

A little later the three of us leave the building, walking arm in arm into the frigid night, and say our goodbyes at the taxi stand. As I am driven home I think about the Professor. He is, to my mind, a hero straight out of Hemingway. Like the old man in our book, the Professor is a man of wisdom, quiet dignity, great courage and resilience. And his wife, too, is a hero. She somehow managed to hold it together throughout the terror-filled months when her family was under threat, and collapsed, essentially, only when they were all out of danger.

The Professor and his family are not listed among the victims of war. His wife is not listed among its casualties. How many tens of thousands more Kosovars "survived" the war, the years of persecution, like this? It has been over a year since the fighting ended, but some wounds are just beginning to surface; some will never heal. The Professor and his family, and countless others in Kosovo, must continue to do what they have already done for so long: Endure.

SATURDAY, MARCH 10, 2001

Our friend Sheryl has packed up her best things and sent them back to the U.S. She is convinced there will be trouble here, and we might have to be evacuated quickly, without our belongings. Ed and I are not concerned. Are we being foolish? I don't think so.

Sheryl has also observed there are fewer young men on the streets these days. Many of them, she thinks, are heading south to the Macedonian border to join the rebels. I agree with her that there is definitely some new, menacing energy in the air.

SUNDAY, MARCH 11, 2001

Robert, a friend in the international police force, CIVPOL, works in the Missing Persons Department, a job, he says, that is the most difficult of his career. He tries to match remains found in mass graves—bones, teeth, pieces of clothing—with descriptions given by the families of the more than three thousand Kosovo Albanians still missing. When a tentative match is made, he takes the remains to the family. Sometimes they can identify a loved one, sometimes they can't. Sometimes, despite overwhelming evidence, the family, the mother or father or wife, refuses to make the identification, refuses to surrender the hope that the missing loved one is not secretly alive in some Serbian jail, refuses to admit the truth. The case that still haunts him, he says, was the man whose brother has been missing since the spring of 1999, and who begged Robert to give him "bones, *any* bones," that he could show to his elderly mother. "Only then can she begin to grieve."

The ground is beginning to thaw, he tells me today, and at least one hundred and fifty unexcavated mass graves lie waiting. In the next few weeks they will start to dig. He isn't looking forward to it.

MONDAY, MARCH 12, 2001

Luan is back from Freiburg, and reports that the metals testing seminar was a great experience. He saw Faton while he was there, and tells me that Faton sends his regards.

I am so glad to see dear Luan. But I hate having to tell him I'm leaving. Really hate it.

Spent some of the afternoon reworking Blerta's résumé. She's applying to the State University of New York at New Paltz, so Sheryl, Ed, and I are helping her get her application together. Afterward, Blerta, Jehona, Sheryl, Ahmet, Ed, and I go out to dinner. I insist on getting to write the thirty-dollar check for her official application fee to SUNY. Something to celebrate! And Blerta will almost certainly be accepted. She is that rare combination of intelligence, ambition, and a kind, generous heart. She's a marvel.

TUESDAY, MARCH 13, 2001

Omar is in charge of the physical plant of the school, and today, on either side of the new school sign, he hangs their new American and British flags. Looking on, Leonard says to me, solemnly, "We would die for your flag, Teacher, just like we would die for our flag."

"Oh, Leonard!" I say, really distressed. "I don't want you to think anymore about dying for my flag or your flag or for anybody's flag. I want you to think about *living!*"

WEDNESDAY, MARCH 14, 2001

What can I do for Leonard? I keep saying to myself, "Maybe if I could . . ." and I follow it with a dozen things I would need to do. Then I realize that the dozen would be only a start. As with most of the young people in Kosovo, lack of money and language are only two of the obstacles he faces. Behind those obstacles lies an ignorance of how the world works, a crippling innocence.

Today he tells me he saw on TV that Michael Jackson is giving money to poor children in America. "Do you think I could write Michael Jackson, Teacher, and ask him to give me some money? I am a poor child, too, only in another country." Or, alternatively, he thinks, there's CNN. "On TV it looks like CNN has a lot of money. Maybe they would give me money to study in the U.S. I could e-mail them."

Like most young men in Kosovo, Leonard spent much of his youth cowering in store entrances, walking down streets hugging the walls, trying to disappear so Serb police wouldn't harass him. The world was divided into two spheres: the warmth and love of his family in their cramped apartment, and the terrors of the streets below. Here is a young man who has spent his whole life trying to be invisible, now trying get someone to take notice of him.

Leonard has never seen a check, a credit card, a business letter, an answering machine, and until we filled out the Soros Foundation application last fall, had never seen an application form. He has never driven a car, been in a taxi, flown on a plane. Were he to be admitted to some university in the U.S., Leonard would not have taxi money to get from his apartment to the Prishtina airport, much less for tuition, room, board, books.

Yet I know that Leonard possesses the courage of heroes. And his capacity for love is limitless. He would die, without hesitation, to protect his mother, his father and sister, and he is willing to work the rest of his life to provide for them. He has lived a life of fear and discrimination and deprivation, yet he refuses to be a victim. Instead, he has developed a quiet dignity, a pride in himself and his family. He is determined to take charge of his life, to take care of those he loves. He would be a treasure for any American university. Leonard *is* a treasure.

I am e-mailing deans at several colleges and universities, telling them about Leonard, asking about aid. In May he will get his test results and hear about his application to the American University in Bulgaria. This would be the perfect solution—a good university close to home. But will it become an option for him? I don't think so. His TOEFL and SAT scores will almost certainly be too low.

THURSDAY, MARCH 15, 2001

Last week at lunch, my policeman friend, Robert, told me an appalling story. Recently, he said, a couple of Christian missionary groups went into two devastated villages in the mountains, telling the villagers (all of whom were Muslims) they were there to help them rebuild. In one village, the missionaries helped build a new well, but when time came to install the pump, much to the villagers' surprise, they were told they must attend Bible class first. In the second village, the missionaries brought in materials and helped the community build a new community center. But before they could get the materials for the roof, the missionaries informed these equally surprised villagers, they must attend a Bible class and prayer meeting. In both these places, the indignant villagers roughed the missionaries up and kicked them out.

I e-mailed this story to an acquaintance back home who is a Methodist minister. "Serves them right!" this spirited woman-of-God writes me today. "Help for these poor war victims should be given unconditionally. They shouldn't have to pay for aid by betraying their religion!"

FRIDAY, MARCH 16, 2001

Amira is going back to Israel today, so it's my last day in class with her. I will miss her quiet intelligence, her kind heart.

With Leonard's family after school for Nora's eleventh birthday. Leonard and I have picked out an electronic keyboard for her as my gift. Nora, Leonard, and I sit on the floor, their parents looking on, and learn to put tunes with percussion. Nora is a natural musician and catches on quickly. The gift is a hit!

Because I was sick the day of the performance and couldn't attend, they show me a video of Nora and her class performing traditional Albanian dances. Then Nora puts on her costume for my admiration. Leonard tells me that until three days before the performance, Nora didn't have a costume; the family couldn't afford it. She had decided she wouldn't dance. But that day, seeing her unhappiness, her father took the bus to Prizren, the cultural center of the country, walked to a traditional clothing shop, put his money ($130) on the counter and said, "Here is my month's salary. I want your best Albanian folk costume for my daughter."

It really is beautiful, and the whole family is so proud of it. Zarife points out every bit of embroidery on the bright green vest, all the colors in the striped apron worn over the long white tunic. This costume is already a family heirloom that carries with it a story of a father's love and a family's sacrifice.

The evening is full of laughter, music. But for me it is shadowed by my conviction, which I keep to myself, that I have failed Leonard, failed the whole family. Sometimes I think that just my presence has raised their expectations, engendered dreams that can never come true.

SATURDAY, MARCH 17, 2001

I take a brief inventory of our clothes and discover many will have to be tossed before we return to the U.S. Our whites have turned gray; our underwear is full of holes. We drink and cook and brush our teeth with bottled water, but our clothes have been subject to local water and detergents.

I learn today that OSCE tells its female employees not to plan to become pregnant until six months after leaving Kosovo. Give their bodies time to get rid of all the toxins, particularly the lead that's in the air.

I am full of tears these days, some shed, some blocked up inside me. I do not want to leave Kosovo.

And I realize that I will be leaving this country never having met a Serb. I have heard stories, read books and articles by and about Serbs in Kosovo and throughout Yugoslavia. But there are only seven hundred or so Serbs still living in Prishtina—out of twenty thousand who were here in June 1999—and they are in hiding, under protection. I have gathered many pieces of the tragic puzzle that is Kosovo, but the picture could never be complete without the pieces held by Serbs.

SUNDAY, MARCH 18, 2001

I pick up worried e-mails from sons and friends today. Are we
O.K.? How dangerous is the situation here? Will there be spill-over
from Macedonia to Kosovo?

And I have to ask myself why I'm not afraid, not even nervous.
Maybe I've become complacent. Maybe I'm blind or just stupid.
Or, maybe there's some part of me that actually likes living on this
kind of edge, close to the border between sanity and insanity, between safety and danger, peace and war.

All those things, probably. But mostly it's my daily experience
with local people here in Prishtina, these sweet, friendly, hospitable
people I've grown to love and care very deeply about. I guess the
biggest part of me believes that we couldn't possibly be hurt in a
place filled with such love.

Yet, have I really just written that? I know, too, that this place is
also filled with hate. And that the love and the hate coexist within
the same people. I see it everywhere.

I know that in my life, I have been spared reasons to hate. It is
only a difference of luck.

MONDAY, MARCH 19, 2001

I have arranged a meeting with Leonard and the Professor. I ask
Leonard to tell the Professor the stories he has heard about incom-
petence and corruption at the university. The Professor, as I had
hoped, reassures Leonard that although that used to be the case—
grades could be bought under Communism, he says—everything
has changed since the war. OSCE and the U.N. are reforming the
university, he says, and are getting rid of corrupt professors and

practices. They are also improving the curriculum and insisting on up-to-date, more student-oriented teaching techniques. It will be a new university, he assures Leonard.

But Leonard is afraid it will all come too late for him. "Things move slowly here," he reminds us. "It will take many years for things to change, and I will not be young then."

When Leonard leaves, I ask the Professor if he will stay in touch with Leonard after I leave. Will he counsel Leonard, give him information and encouragement? See that he gets through the university registration process? The Professor promises he will do that. I feel better.

TUESDAY, MARCH 20, 2001

There are more books at the Cambridge School now, the beginnings of a library. There are space heaters in the classrooms, and posters, tables, and chairs in the lobby. It looks more and more like a real school.

And in the city, more helicopter gunships overhead. All hell has broken loose in Macedonia. More Kosovo Albanians slip across the border every day, eager to fight. Leaders from the U.N., NATO, and the European Union fly in and out of Skopje trying to calm things down, and people here in Kosovo, on the streets, in the shops, in the international offices, are edgy. Is this the beginning of another Balkan conflagration?

WEDNESDAY, MARCH 21, 2001

In our conversation class last week I asked each student to practice giving instructions about something they know how to do. Fatmira told us how to make coffee; the Professor told us how to make *better* coffee; Drita told us how to make an apple pie; and Emina told us how to get rid of a boyfriend you don't like anymore! First, you try to show him with your attitude, then you start telling him what's wrong with him, then . . .

Relating this to Ed last night, he remarked, laughing, that it sounded like Paul Simon's "Fifty Ways to Leave Your Lover." What a clever man my husband is! I had just bought the CD from a street vendor downtown.

So, today I come with the CD player and speakers, and give each student a page with part of the lyrics, but with the "ways" left blank. They have to listen and write them down. An unusual dictation exercise, but after a while the whole class is rockin'! We all sing along with Paul Simon:

> You just slip out the back, Jack
> Make a new plan, Stan
> You don't need to be coy, Roy
> Just get yourself free!

FRIDAY, MARCH 23, 2001
Our last class

They wanted a party, of course. Granit 2 and Edona have brought Cokes and cookies. And there are presents: the Cambridge School presents me with a plaque, a copper engraving of the map of Kosovo. The Professor has brought me cups for Turkish coffee. And from the younger students: a spritely ceramic duck, three plastic music boxes, a wooden vase from Luan, a vase made of snail shells from Drita. We laugh and joke and take pictures. I remark that Besart seems to have grown six inches since we started the course!

But as we sit down at our long table together for the last time, they are suddenly quiet. I look around and can tell they expect me to make a speech. These students, like most Kosovars I've met, have a strong sense of propriety; they enjoy tradition, ceremony, formal courtesies. Clearly, they believe the proper thing for this occasion is for Teacher to say some last words, to provide a punctuation mark to our many months together.

I am caught off guard. For a couple of weeks I've been asking myself: What is it, beyond a better knowledge of the English language, I would like to leave with my students? I've talked with Ed about it. Years from now, when I'm a white-haired old lady in my rocking chair reminiscing about my time teaching in Kosovo, what will I wish I had said to them? Surely there's something I believe, something important I want to impart. But I could never think of anything that didn't sound melodramatic or self-righteous or just downright sentimental. So I had decided to make no last remarks.

And now, I am being called upon to say something. Something serious.

Drita, Genti, Leonard, Luan, Leutrim, the two Granits, Besart, Edona, Fazile, Fatmira, Emina, the Professor. They are waiting for me. And suddenly it comes to me. I remember the Buddha's precept of right speech, and I know that that is what I want to talk about.

I don't mention the Buddha, of course, as some have probably never heard of him. But I tell them about the idea, as I understand it. For several months, I say, we've been learning how to speak English correctly. Correct grammar, appropriate vocabulary. But there is more to think about than the correctness of the language. We all have a responsibility to think about the purpose of language— what we *do* with our words. I encourage you to use your new language to try to understand people who are different from you, to help them understand you. And use your new words to say kind things to one another, to help other people, to encourage them, to make them feel better about themselves. To express the things I know each of you feels in your heart: love, generosity, compassion.

And, I say at the end, use your English to e-mail your Teacher! Everyone laughs.

It does sound both sentimental and pretentious as I write it tonight—as I had feared. But as I looked around this afternoon I could see that they were pleased. The little speech had met their expectations, satisfied their sense of propriety, and with some, maybe touched a chord or two. They now felt there had been a proper close to our time together. And the Professor had smiled at me and nodded. I think he, too, approved.

Tuesday, March 27, 2001

We are packing for vacation, trying to pack light, leaving everything here we're not absolutely sure we will use in Italy. I run across my worn and tattered copy of *The Old Man and the Sea*. It's a slight book, a little paperback of only a hundred pages, and I've been carrying it in my purse for months now, since we formed the book club. I leaf through it, trying to decide whether it goes with us to Italy. Every page is cluttered with my marginalia in pencil and various colors of ink—ideas for book club discussions scribbled at the top margins, notes about symbolism at the bottom. Particularly wonderful passages—those I decided to read aloud to the group — are underlined and exclamation-marked. The title page, fly leaves, and inside covers are filled with summaries of our book club meetings, and dozens of little bits of paper are stuck between the pages, hastily scribbled notes about daily conversations and events that I transferred to my diary each night.

It still seems like a miracle that of all the books in the world to find in Prishtina, Kosovo, after the war, I found this one. I remember when I first spotted the book I was worried about Hemingway's machismo—what Virginia Woolf called his "self-conscious virility." But *The Old Man and the Sea* turned out to be the perfect work of literature for these students, for our book club. Short, with straightforward prose they could read and understand, and the story—well. Hemingway's fable of the spirit's victory over loss and adversity turned out to be the story of my students' lives.

I pack the old man carefully in a corner of my suitcase. He will go with us to Italy.

MONDAY, APRIL 2, 2001
Lucca, Italy

Ed and I are here for some R&R—the best kind: the steep wooded hills south of Lucca, the slow, dignified pace of the medieval walled town, and in Florence, the buildings, the art of the Renaissance. Civilization, yes? Yes, but . . . On the wall of the fourteenth-century building across from our internet café, graffiti exclaiming *"Albanesi merde!"* Albanians are shit. And one of the first things our landlord, Bruno, told us when showing us our rented apartment was to beware of Albanians and Moroccans who would come down from the hills and steal us blind.

"How can we recognize Albanians?" asked Ed, innocently.

"They are *dark,*" declared Bruno, who is himself darker than any Albanian we have ever met, "and they are *brutal!*"

"And have you ever seen any of these swarthy brigands in the neighborhood?" Ed continues, barely able to contain himself.

Well, no, not exactly. No one had, really.

But the Albanian diaspora is immense. There are thousands here in Italy working to send money back to their families in Kosovo and Albania. And here—as in Serbia, Macedonia, Bulgaria, Greece—they are often feared and despised.

We have just come from the Balkans, an area of the world that has come to symbolize savagery and divisiveness. But as I think again about the history of Italy, I am reminded that the charming hill towns, these towers and castles and graceful walls—the principal *attractions* of Tuscany—were built because for hundreds of years Italians hated and tortured and raped and killed each other. The history of Italian city-states makes the Balkans look like the Peaceable Kingdom.

WEDNESDAY, APRIL 4, 2001

I remember when Ed first said he wanted to go to Kosovo, I complained, half-joking, "Why couldn't you go reform the legal system in Tuscany?"

And now we're in Tuscany, and I cannot get Kosovo out of my mind. Some of my students have obtained e-mail addresses, and when they can get some time on one of the school's few computers, or get together some money for an internet café, they contact me. I hear the despair in what Emina writes me today from the computer at her job: "Please don't forget us, Teacher. Remember that we Kosovar students have the worst luck in the world with our teaching, our traditions, our living—everything. I think that God forgot us. Please don't you forget us."

THURSDAY, APRIL 5, 2001

Leonard e-mails today that he did as I had told him to do. Despite his shyness, he dragged himself to the new American Center at the university library and, being "politely pushy" as we had practiced, got the attention of one of the counselors. "I spoke good English to him and he and everyone around was surprised," he writes proudly. Good for Leonard! I'm so proud of him! The counselor gave Leonard a lot of time and promised he would help him apply to American universities and look for financial aid.

And of course, I will continue to help him.

Before we left for Italy, Ed and I gave Leonard enough money to allow him to keep pursuing his educational goals for a while— classes, web searches, books, tutoring. We will send him more as we can afford it. But we all know it's only a drop in the bucket.

Every effort in Kosovo is merely a drop in the bucket.

THURSDAY, APRIL 12, 2001

Ah, Tuscany!

WEDNESDAY, APRIL 18, 2001
Prishtina, Kosovo

The Professor and I made an appointment to meet at a café down-town. I wanted him to meet Ed, and I wanted to say goodbye. To-day Ed and I wait for forty-five minutes, then leave. I know there was a mix-up over time or place. I phone him later. He had waited for me at the school, he says. I can tell he is as upset as I am, though he says only, "Ah, well, Mrs. Paula . . ." Tonight I am distraught. I wanted to see him today. And I know, of course, that what I am really upset about is that I probably won't see the Professor, or any of my students, ever again.

FRIDAY, APRIL 20, 2001

A car-bombing today in front of the Yugoslav passport office on Mother Teresa Boulevard. One Serb killed, three injured, murderers unknown. So many things seem to be unraveling here: Fanatical Albanians killing Serbs, Roma, and other minorities; more political squabbling among the Albanian parties; more uncertainties about the elections; escalating ethnic hostilities in Macedonia. It just keeps getting harder—for everyone.

TUESDAY, APRIL 24, 2001

We have said our goodbyes to the wonderful local staff in Ed's office. Hajriz and Fexhi, Ardita and Ahmet, Arbin, Albin, and Fadil. And to Jehona and Blerta—how can we live without them now? I've walked up the street saying goodbye to the merchants I've come to know; Fatmir has presented me with a bottle of his best Albanian brandy and lets me take his picture in front of his chocolate candies. At the internet café next to the Grand Hotel I've shaken Osman's hand for the last time, telling him how much I've appreciated his courtesy and his tips on pronunciation. Igballe and I have hugged and cried. And although Isa tries to hide it, I know he is worried about their income; with so many internationals leaving, will he be able to rent the house again?

Since my class ended I haven't had the heart to write much in my journal. But tomorrow, after eight months abroad, we leave Kosovo for good, so I feel I should write something. My fingers are stumbling around on the keyboard, though, and my mind is leaping about, not knowing where to land.

I remember a letter my brother, David, wrote me not long ago—a long thoughtful letter about the futility of most human efforts to improve things. Humanity evolves at its own speed, he says, and we are a long way away from being anywhere close to goodness, kindness, peace. He worries, I think, that with all the renewed violence in the area, I am discouraged, unhappy with our decision to come here. Maybe, he thinks, I have become cynical. After all, things look less stable now than they did when we arrived eight months ago.

It is true that after seeing what I have seen, learning what I have learned, I am less hopeful than ever about our human condition. I doubt we can ever straighten ourselves out. World peace is only a dream. The most we can do, I fear, is to prevent violence in some places, put a lid on it in others, help each other when we can.

But in the place of hope I now feel . . . something else. I look around me and see that most of us share a certain sweetness. Most of us are trying to live decent lives, doing what we can for our families and children, trying to find some meaning, to piece together the puzzle. But we keep blundering, stumbling, falling into fits of rage and fear, hatred and self-destruction. Our stories are often sad, tragic, maddening. And I am not hopeful that things will get much better. I don't see progress, but I don't feel cynicism. I feel only an immense tenderness for all of us.

Tonight, as I have often done during my stay in Kosovo, I turn to a copy of *The Sun,* the magazine published by my friend, Sy. In an interview, James Hillman advises us to "pick one place where your heart can connect to the world's problems."

For me, that place has been Kosovo. I am so very lucky to have found it.

Tomorrow, home.

Saturday, May 5, 2001
Bolinas, California

Back to our little house on the cliff overlooking the blue and sparkling ocean. San Francisco is still there where we left it, spread out on the coast south of us, looking clean and white and beautiful. The malls of Marin County—one of the two wealthiest counties in the nation—are still there, too. We shopped for a few things yesterday.

I do love being back in our house, with our books and music and funny Rodney, our cat. I love being able to pick up the phone and call my parents, our sons, my friends. And I hadn't realized how much I missed the color blue. Now I can see it every day—changing shades of it in the ocean below us.

I walk down the street to the point, where Duxbury Reef begins and the egrets and herons feed, and I don't encounter a single piece of trash. The air is fresh, salty, pure, without a whiff of rotting vegetables. A fishing boat lies off the reef, and in the distance I see a white Princess Cruise liner on its way into the Golden Gate.

But I feel so sad, so lost. *Where am I? What am I doing here?*

We are both disoriented. I am close to depression. I miss Kosovo. I miss Igballe and Isa, Jehona and Blerta. I miss the shopkeepers on our street, Fatmir, Orhan, Lulje. And I miss my students. I yearn for them.

I've gotten e-mail greeting cards from Emina, Genti, Leutrim, and both Granits. They say they miss me. And Leonard is e-mailing almost every day. The connection is still there with those who have e-mail. Will I be able to maintain it? I am so far away.

FRIDAY, JUNE 15, 2001

Ed and I sit on our deck this evening, watching the full moon rise over Bolinas Ridge, reflected in the calm waters of the bay. We talk about how our family seems to have expanded. Jehona and Blerta call us Mom and Dad, and we consider them our "adopted daughters." Leonard speaks of me as his "American mother" and I call him my "Kosovar son." Emina and Fatmira address me as "dear Teacher, dear friend, dear sister."

Jehona and Blerta are flying to the U.S. in August for special legal training Ed has arranged for them. They will attend our son Paul's wedding in Baltimore with us, then fly back to California to stay with us for a couple of weeks. Jehona's brother, Besnik, will join us for part of that time.

I read to Ed the e-mail I got today from Faton, who is in Tirana, Albania, trying to get a German visa to continue his physics studies in Jena. He writes that when he was in Germany he saw "the difference between the West and my country is very big. I ask myself: When will we Kosovars build our country and learn to work like people of the West?

"Dear Teacher, I think very often of you. You teach me the English language and what is more *important* for me I learn from you how to respect work, how Americans work, how to be closer with people. (This is important for me because I am young and am constructing my identity.) Dear Teacher, I will consider you my teacher for all my life."

I don't understand all this, I tell Ed. But something magical happened for me in Kosovo. Some combination of circumstance, time, and place made possible an extraordinary relationship between my students and me, a relationship that feels now like a bond. I know it is the fate of the teacher to be left behind, even forgotten. But because of the remarkable character of these Kosovar students, because of their openness, their warm and generous hearts, perhaps because of what they have endured, they seem to want me to stay in their lives, not just as a symbol of a better world, but as a real, human presence.

Chance and my husband's desire to help sent me to Kosovo, to the middle of the Balkans, after a tragic war. I am an ordinary American woman who was given an extraordinary opportunity, and, in a way, my students seized that opportunity for themselves, making me into what they needed. I offered only ordinary stuff, the love and encouragement we all have to offer, but they were in short supply in Kosovo. These students possess their own youthful optimism, but, after fifty years of Communism, apartheid, war, there is little in their society that signals back to them, that says, "Yes, go for it! You can do it!" I was lucky enough to be able to love and encourage them full time for many months.

My dream returned last night, the dream I've had since I ended my brief teaching career in my early twenties. I am standing in a classroom preparing to teach students who want to learn, and I am filled with happiness. I awoke thinking, What teacher, even in her dreams, could have imagined such a rewarding experience as I had in Kosovo? I know that some part of me will always be in that classroom in the burned-out Sports Center in Prishtina.

MONDAY, JUNE 18, 2001

My sister-in-law writes that she visited the Hemingway-Pfeiffer home, recently converted to a museum and education center, close to my hometown in Arkansas. The home of his second wife, Pauline, this is where Hemingway often stayed and wrote short stories and some of *A Farewell to Arms*. Linda told the museum officials about the Hemingway Book Club of Kosova. They have asked me to send a photograph of club members, some teaching materials, and a letter with the club logo. They'll display it in the house museum. I can't wait to e-mail club members about this. They will be thrilled! Who would have thought it?

FRIDAY, FEBRUARY 1, 2002

Soon after we returned home in the summer of 2001, Leonard e-mailed me, asking that I review a draft of an inquiry letter he planned to e-mail to American colleges. In the letter I could hear his anxious but determined voice:

Dear Dean,
My name is Leonard. . . . I am nineteen years old and live in Kosovo. I know that America is a place of opportunities and I really wish I could have a chance to try one of them. I want to study economics and business and hopefully come back to Kosovo one day and use my education to build new institutions in my country.
Unfortunately, the war made us very poor so my family

cannot pay my expenses. I need a scholarship to realize my dream. Please help me.

Today, nine months after we left Kosovo, I sit at my computer e-mailing colleges about Leonard. We still haven't been able to figure out a way to get him to school in the U.S. His TOEFL score last year wasn't high enough to qualify him for the American University in Bulgaria—so we lost that battle. And we are finding that most American colleges offer virtually no large scholarships or grants to foreign students for undergraduate study. Quite the contrary. Many U.S. colleges count on the high out-of-state tuitions paid by wealthy foreign families. Foreign families with little money, like Leonard's, are out of luck.

But although he is occasionally discouraged, Leonard never stops trying. I see in all his communications a new self-confidence, a growing certainty of his own worth and potential. He is studying to take the TOEFL again and has researched and contacted some two dozen American colleges and universities. All this while he is making excellent grades in economics and management at the University of Prishtina. Leonard has become a dynamo!

Because the Professor doesn't have e-mail, Leonard acts as our courier. In reply to my concern about his wife, the Professor tells me she no longer recognizes him or their sons. It is clear her war-wounded mind is sinking deeper into darkness. Leonard says the Professor looks very, very tired, but is friendly and helpful, as always, and sends "Mrs. Paula" his best regards.

Leutrim, the Granits, Genti, Besart, and Edona—the now-sixteen-year-olds—e-mail me often about their English-language studies. Leutrim says: "I made an excellent score on the Upper Intermediate exam. It is because of you, Teacher. I don't think there will be any other one who can learn me as much as you did. And I miss you a lot." They write of their hopes for careers in architecture, medicine, law: professions, they believe, their developing country will require. Four of the boys will apply this spring to the Soros Foundation to take a year of high school in the U.S., and I will write recommendations for them. But there are hundreds of worthy applicants, and few available slots. If they can't get to the U.S. with the Soros program, we'll need to find another way.

Faton is now studying for his Ph.D. at a university in Germany. His frequent e-mails are ecstatic. The university, he says, has "excellent working conditions, as I dreamed, and I'm working very hard because this is my great chance for me to continue my journey through science."

Luan is still trying to find a way to work on his Ph.D. in mechanical engineering in the U.S. or Western Europe. Although he hasn't yet gotten the big break he needs, he is optimistic. "I have ever believed in the future, Teacher," he reminds me. "I will succeed."

Emina has been promoted, and now monitors several projects. In her usual feisty way, she writes that some of her employees consider her to be too "strict," but "it is my responsibility, I tell them! They must give me what I need so I can do my job!" She sounds strong, self-assured, and happy. But she never mentions her cousin, Fatmira, and since Fatmira doesn't use e-mail, I wonder—and worry—about her. Has she been able to finish high school? Is she O.K.?

Drita, lovely, shy Drita, doesn't use e-mail, either. But Leonard saw her not long ago on the university campus and tells me she is studying English as a freshman now. She still wants to teach English or, maybe, become a translator. She sends me her love, Leonard says.

Jehona and Blerta, Ed's beloved assistants, charge ahead in their inimitable ways. Jehona continues to work as a legal assistant at ABA-CEELI and Blerta is studying international relations at the State University of New York, on a rare scholarship. Blerta calls us each week and visits us during her vacations.

✐

At the end of July 2001, three months after we returned, my father died. My students all responded with condolences, including Granit 2's plea to "keep yourself and be strong." It was a sad irony that my father's funeral took place on the same day as my stepson Paul's wedding. When I returned to our coastal home after the funeral, Jehona and Blerta, fresh from the wedding I could not attend, were waiting to comfort me. Their love, and their understanding of loss, helped me through that difficult time.

Shortly thereafter, when the ghastly pictures of the World Trade Center and the Pentagon hit Kosovo television, I was immediately deluged with worried e-mails. Emina wrote from her desk at work: "I just heard what happened in New York. Please send me an e-mail are you and your relatives O.K.? Teacher, I'm very worried about you. Please only tell me you are O.K."

Jehona's mother, Feride, who works at Prishtina's Red Cross, reported that thousands of Kosovars tried to donate blood for victims in New York and Washington. The lines in front of their office were so long, she said, the Red Cross had to turn people away. "We had not enough freezers for all the blood our people would give to Americans."

My students wrote me of their shock, their sorrow. Leonard wrote: "We are with you. I, my family, my country are shocked because our friends are attacked. Paula, I cried, my heart cried, too. I saw those bad photos and I remembered our country two years before. We Albanians know how you Americans feel now. I know it is hard. We are sorry about it because America is part of our history. We are with you."

He and his father attended a Christian church service, he wrote later, and "prayed for America." The Americans at the service, he said, "thanked us a lot for being there with them."

Two months later, on November 11, 2001, the first democratic national elections were held in Kosovo. Because the moderate Albanian party, the LDK, headed by Ibrahim Rugova, didn't receive a clear majority, compromise with two more radical parties headed by former KLA leaders became necessary. As I write this today, the rival Albanian parties are still deadlocked, unable to form a government. When I asked the students recently what they thought of this power struggle, Genti reminded me that "when you started America many of your leaders didn't get along. Look at America now!" And Granit 2, as is his wont, stated the obvious: "Democracy is not as easy as it looks, Teacher."

Despite its problems, this election seems to have become the defining event in a new, emerging national consciousness. Hope has become conviction. Kosovo Albanians are beginning to believe— really believe—that Kosovo is on its way to becoming an independent nation. And despite all evidence to the contrary, they believe prosperity is just around the corner. Luan's recent message echoes the feelings of many of his countrymen: "Now we can know for sure the Serbs will not oppress us again. We can build our economy and have a free country. It will happen!"

Many Kosovars are becoming impatient with UNMIK's refusal to hand over more power to Kosovar leaders, and its refusal to act more quickly on the issue of Kosovo's political status. These Kosovars want independence, *now!* A disgruntled Kosovar friend e-mailed me recently, "Why should internationals want Kosova to rule itself? UNMIK employees are earning a hundred thousand euros a year to stay here and boss us around!"

Other Kosovars, though, seem to be still grateful for UNMIK's presence, and believe the U.N., the U.S., and the European Union have Kosovo's best interests at heart. They will wait.

The question is, what lies at the end of the waiting? What will Kosovo's political status be? Independence? Serbia will fight it. Will it become in fact what it actually still is, a province of Serbia? This is what the Kosovo Serb minority hopes for, but Kosovo Albanians will never accept it, no matter how much autonomy they are promised. Or will it remain indefinitely a de facto colony of the United Nations? No one likes this alternative.

The United Nations' new administrator in Kosovo, Michael Steiner, states often and unequivocally that the future political status of Kosovo won't even be *discussed* until Kosovo meets certain standards, including the reduction of crime, the stabilization of governing institutions, the creation of more jobs, and, critically, the creation of a multiethnic society.

Certainly, progress has already been made in many of these areas. Over $2 billion in reconstruction monies, mostly from the EU, have poured into Kosovo since the war. Roads have been resurfaced and thousands of houses have been rebuilt. Plans are being made for privatizating Kosovo's state-owned companies, an essential step toward developing a market economy. Leutrim writes me that Prishtina is being cleaned up and there is "more grass in some places." Many of the downtown buildings are being painted in soft Mediterranean pastels, he says, and an enormous new equestrian statue of Skanderbeg has been erected on Mother Teresa Boulevard. He is so proud of the changes, he has put together a website about "Prishtina, My City."

But the average family in Kosovo still earns only enough to buy food for one week of each month. Sixty-five percent of the population is unemployed and 70 percent lives in deep poverty. Half the cars in the country are stolen and corruption is rampant. Organized crime, including smuggling (all those stolen cars), drug trafficking, and trafficking in women, threaten not only public safety but also the fragile economy.

And the awful truth is, even if they can get the education they need, there are no jobs for bright young people like Leonard, Leutrim, Genti, Drita, and the Granits. In a country with virtually no manufacturing, financial institutions, or international trade, who will hire MBAs, engineers, accountants, and lawyers? In a country of people who can't afford bread, who will hire architects? Recently, a spokesman for the economics faculty at the university stated that Kosovo won't be able to employ even a fraction of the many students now studying economics at the university, adding, cynically, that at least their studies keep them off the streets for now. Did Leonard, now studying economics, hear this, I wonder?

Our Balkans news sources report progress being made for Kosovar women—with seats in the Assembly designated for women, and new organizations that provide remedial education and vocational training, as well as counseling for victims of domestic abuse.

Recent news reports tell another story. In a mountain village, a young woman was married to the son of a neighboring family. The morning after the wedding, the son's family brought the girl back to her parents, rejected, perhaps, because she wasn't a virgin. UNMIK police have arrested two of her male relatives who, they contend, shot her many times and buried her secretly. In that same week, in another part of the country, a young woman went to live with her boyfriend and his family, something not done in that part of the world. Her brother followed her to the boyfriend's home and shot her dead. The Kanun of Lek raises its ugly head again.

There may be a new day for women in Kosovo, but I fear that day won't dawn anytime soon, and, as always, the rural areas will remain in the medieval dark, perhaps for generations.

Of all of Kosovo's many challenges, surely the most daunting is the creation of a society in which Albanians, Serbs, and other ethnic groups can live together peacefully. There are estimates that as many as 200,000 to 250,000 Serbs, Roma, and other minorities who fled Kosovo after the war remain as refugees, mostly in Serbia. The U.N. says these refugees must be allowed to return to their homes without harm, and that there will be no discussion of Kosovo's future status until this occurs.

Many observers think ethnic passions are subsiding. It is hoped that the war crimes trial of Slobodan Milosevic at the International Criminal Tribunal for the Former Yugoslavia, deemed the "trial of the century" and scheduled to begin February 12, 2002, will do much to persuade victims that at least some justice is being done. And Kosovo Albanian leaders are saying the correct, conciliatory words, repeating the U.N. mantra, "multiethnic, multicultural."

But the fact remains: A few acts of vengeance are all it will take to stop the returns, to defeat integration and multiethnicity, to destroy the hope of a prosperous, independent Kosovo. For without integration, there will be no decision about political status, and while its political status is still in limbo, what entrepreneur will be willing to risk capital in Kosovo?

So everything depends upon the safe return and integration of the "enemy." After all they've been through, can Kosovo Albanians manage this? There are still thousands of scores to be settled in a country with a long, bloody tradition of score-settling.

Yet, as I write this today, I remember the energy, the enthusiasm, the can-do attitude of my students. And I think of the exuberant messages they still send me regularly, messages full of plans for the future. I know that the Professor, Luan and Faton, Leonard, Drita, the Granits, Edona, Emina, and the others have freed themselves of what historian Julie Mertus deems the most dangerous identity one can adopt: the identity as victim. If we become "steeped in our own victimhood," Mertus says, "we no longer feel bound by moral considerations in becoming perpetrators." Although they *are* victims, of course, of terrible oppression and brutality, these students are not wasting their time on notions of revenge or self-pity. They are concentrating instead on their roles as students, as future entrepreneurs and professionals, as builders of their country. If optimism is the highest form of courage—as I am beginning to believe it is—then these students are all heroes.

George Santayana's much-quoted warning—"Those who cannot remember the past are condemned to repeat it"—must be turned on its head in Kosovo. It is because of Serbs' and Albanians' *obsession* with the past—and with the myths that masquerade as the past—that they seem condemned continually to repeat it. No, the issue in Kosovo is this: How many Kosovars have, like my students, the will to let go of the past, to set aside the wrongs that have been done to them and focus instead on the necessities of the present and the possibilities of the future? How many are willing to draw a line between past and present, and simply take a step forward?

Only yesterday Faton wrote me, "I think the people of Kosova will understand that the only way to enjoy life and to be incorporated in Western societies is by work, love for human beings, tolerance, respect for each other, and looking toward the future."

And I remember what the Professor told me once: "Forgiveness takes courage. But we *have* courage. We *can* live together."

Although it is the European nations that must bear the principal responsibility for reconstruction and peace-keeping in Kosovo, the importance of America's role cannot be overestimated. And this is partly for reasons that are psychological and symbolic. America is a mythic place for many Kosovo Albanians. Not only is it the country that, with Britain, led NATO in driving out the Serb military, but it is also the place of their dreams. Kosovo Albanians believe in America's sympathy for their cause. They see America as their natural ally, the country that, more than any other, understands their struggle for independence. Americans and Kosovars, they believe, have a special affinity for one another and share important values: courage, individual initiative, and love of freedom. But the sad truth is that while Kosovo Albanians think of America every day, Americans have almost forgotten Kosovo.

Before Ed and I went to Kosovo I never paid much attention to our government's foreign policy, to what we were doing in the Balkans or anywhere else. But now I am vigilant. Now I have seen the faces of those on the receiving end of American foreign policy. I have seen the taxi drivers, the shopkeepers, the professors, the students, the housewives, the children whose entire lives are changed, and changed forever by the decisions made in the White House, the state department, the Congress of the United States.

I know now that if America pulls its support out of Kosovo— not just peacekeeping support, but economic support and support for their long-term institution building, as well—it will hurt Leonard and his family, the Professor and his wife, Leutrim, Faton, Drita, Emina, Luan, the Granits, Genti, and Besart—it will hurt all of them.

Today, as a new year is underway, it is no longer enough to sit at my computer and receive e-mails from Kosovo. I want to *see* my students again. I want to hug Leonard and sit with his family in their small parlor with its "NATO splinter." I want to hear more of the Professor's wise words and find out about his wife. I want to see how the sixteen-year-olds have grown. I want to see what I can do to help Luan get to the U.S. for graduate school. I want to discover whether Emina and Fatmira are indeed, as they had hoped, establishing independent lives for themselves. I want to hear Drita's gentle voice again and try to find Fazile and the other students I've lost track of. And I want to see Isa, Igballe, and Agim. Because they don't have e-mail, I've completely lost touch with them. Were they able to rent our flat? Is Isa working again? Have they been able to stay in their home?

Ed has recently published an article describing the grim prospects for Kosovo's legal system, and is eager to return to investigate the situation further. And we both want to see for ourselves what Kosovo looks like, feels like two and a half years after the end of the war. We both know that Kosovo is more than a place where we lived for eight months. Kosovo is a commitment.

So, we will return this spring. We will stay with Jehona and her family while I connect again with my students. When I e-mailed them of the possibility of returning for a visit, Leutrim and Leonard wrote back immediately volunteering to try to round everyone up for a class reunion at the Cambridge School. And Genti wrote: "We wonder why anyone would come back to Kosova. We think you must love us very much."

I've already begun to think of presents to take—*The Complete Short Stories of Ernest Hemingway* for everyone, and maybe English translations of their great Albanian writer, Ismail Kadare, whose works I have grown to love. Ed suggests that I have T-shirts made with a picture of a marlin leaping from the sea and the words, "The Hemingway Book Club of Kosova" emblazoned on the front. The students will love it.

Last spring when we left Kosovo, I worried that the bonds between my students and me might not hold. And I wondered what, if anything, of all our time together, would survive in their memories? I was so happy to find that, from the beginning, my students stayed in touch, continuing to involve me in their lives, and offering me love and comfort when I needed it most.

And then, last week, I e-mailed all of them:

In today's newspaper I noticed a headline that says, "Hemingway's Boat Captain Dead at 104." A man named Gregorio

Fuentes, the man Hemingway used as a model for Santiago, the old fisherman in *The Old Man and the Sea,* died two days ago in a small town on the coast of Cuba where he had been a fisherman his whole life. He was 104 years old. He had taken Hemingway out fishing in the ocean many times in the 1930s and '40s, and Hemingway was very fond of him.

Do you remember Hemingway's description? "Everything about him was old except his eyes, and they were the same color as the sea and were cheerful and undefeated." Do you remember the old man?

Today, I am beginning to receive their responses. Yes, they say. They, too, saw the story on the BBC and thought of the old man, of Hemingway, of our book club. Yes, they tell me. They remember.

The first meeting of the Hemingway Book Club of Kosova, Fall 2000.

APPENDIX

INTERNATIONAL VOLUNTEER OPPORTUNITIES

There are literally thousands of opportunities available to Americans who wish to volunteer for service abroad. Some organizations that sponsor volunteers, like the Peace Corps, are well-known. However, there are hundreds of other lesser-known but excellent organizations that offer volunteer positions in areas such as humanitarian relief, education, peace-building and human-rights promotion, community development and vocational training. Interesting and important jobs exist for older teens through older adults, and range in terms of commitment from a few weeks to a few years. (Most non-governmental organizations, I should point out, charge program/placement fees to participants.)

Because it would require another book to list and describe all of the volunteer organizations, I have presented below only a few whose websites offer both useful general information on international volunteering and links to many other organizations. When you log on to the websites below and follow the links, you will be able to find every conceivable kind of volunteer opportunity in countries around the globe. I have also provided the phone numbers and addresses of most of these organizations for those of you who are not "on-line."

I have had no personal experience with any of these organizations, and offer them to you for your own exploration and discovery.

Action Without Borders' website presents links to 28,000 nonprofit and community organizations offering volunteer opportunities.

Action Without Borders, Inc.
79 Fifth Avenue, 17th Floor
New York, NY 10003
(212) 843-3973
www.Idealist.org

AFS, formerly American Field Service, lists on its website exchange opportunities for students, young adults, and teachers in fifty countries. The website also offers excellent links to other organizations, especially in the field of education.

AFS International
71 W. 23rd Street, 17th Floor
New York, NY 10010
(212) 807-8686
www.AFS.org

Council Exchanges is a leader in student exchange programs and also offers short-term, team-oriented international volunteer programs.

Council Exchanges
633 Third Avenue
New York, NY 10017
(888) COUNCIL
www.us.councilexchanges.org

Cross-Cultural Solutions, an independent, nonreligious nonprofit organization, sends over 1,000 volunteers overseas every year.

Cross-Cultural Solutions
47 Potter Avenue
New Rochelle, NY 10801
(800) 380-4777
www.crossculturalsolutions.org

Global Volunteers has mobilized more than 13,000 volunteers on human and economic development projects worldwide.

Global Volunteers
375 East Little Canada Road
St. Paul, MN 55117-1628
(800) 487-1074
(651) 407-6100
www.globalvolunteers.org

Habitat for Humanity is a nondenominational Christian service organization that has built houses in more than eighty countries for those in need of adequate shelter.

Habitat for Humanity
Partner Service Center
121 Habitat Street

Americus, GA 31709
(229) 924-6935
www.habitat.org

Interaction, American Council for Voluntary International Action is a coalition of 150 U.S.–based nonprofits working in 165 countries. The website offers extensive links.

Interaction
1717 Massachusetts Avenue NW, Suite 701
Washington, DC 20036
(202) 667-8236
www.Interaction.org

The International Year of Volunteers 2001 was designated by the United Nations General Assembly to provide a favorable environment for the growth and strategic use of volunteers of all kinds. Follow the links on this excellent site to learn information about thousands of volunteer organizations—both related and unrelated to the U.N.—throughout the world.
www.iyv2001.org

International Volunteer Programs Association is an excellent search site for international volunteers and internship opportunities.
www.volunteerinternational.org

OneWorld US is the American division of OneWorld International, a community of over 1,250 organizations working for social justice. The website offers extensive information about issues and needs throughout the world, and lists volunteer posts in human rights, environmental programs, and sustainable development projects.

OneWorld US
Benton Foundation
1625 K Street NW, 11th Floor
Washington, DC 20006
(202) 638-5770
www.oneworld.net

The **Peace Corps,** founded by President John F. Kennedy, offers a website with a comprehensive overview of the volunteer experience, as well as information about specific opportunities.

Peace Corps
The Paul D. Coverdell Peace Corps Headquarters
1111 20th Street NW
Washington, DC 20526
(800) 424-8580
www.peacecorps.gov

The American Friends Service Committee is a Quaker organization that includes people of various faiths who are committed to social justice, peace, and humanitarian service.

AFSC
1501 Cherry Street
Philadelphia, PA 19102
(215) 241-7000
www.afsc.org

The United Nations Volunteers Program (UNV), administered by the United Nations Development Program, supports human development throughout the world by encouraging volunteerism.
www.unvolunteers.org

Volunteer Abroad offers one of the largest directories on the internet, including links to small, grassroots organizations.

GoAbroad.com
8 East First Avenue, Suite 102
Denver, CO 80203
(720) 570-1702
www.VolunteerAbroad.com

TEACHING ENGLISH TO SPEAKERS OF OTHER LANGUAGES

Many people in developing countries want and need to learn English in order to more effectively participate in the global community. Teachers of English to Speakers of Other Languages (TESOL) is the professional organization for teachers in the field. TESOL's excellent website offers information about the field of study and the profession, as well as educational and career opportunities.

TESOL
700 South Washington Street, Suite 200
Alexandria, VA 22314
(703) 836-0774
www.tesol.org

ACKNOWLEDGMENTS

I could never adequately express my thanks to my students for their many kindnesses, and for the inspiration they continue to provide to me every day. I can only hope that as they read this journal, they will begin to understand my love for them, and my deep gratitude.

I am forever indebted to Lorraine Kisly, who, upon reading my e-mailed journal entries, asked if I would let her "find a home" for the diary. She succeeded in finding the perfect home at Jeremy P. Tarcher/Putnam when Sara Carder expressed her enthusiasm for these stories from Kosovo. So, to Lorraine, my agent, and to Sara, my editor, I say thank you. I know that for you, too, *The Hemingway Book Club of Kosovo* has been a labor of love.

I would also like to thank the administration of McGeorge School of Law, University of the Pacific, for having granted my husband, Ed Villmoare, a leave of absence so we could go to Kosovo. Thanks, too, to Ceri Rich-Odeh of the Transworld Schools in San Francisco, for offering me a scholarship when she discovered I was headed for Kosovo. Ceri and her excellent staff taught me the basics of teaching English as a second language, and gave me the confidence to return to the classroom. And many thanks to the management and staff of The Cambridge School in Prishtina. I will always remember your unfailing courtesy and support.

Thank you to all my family and friends who encouraged me to go to Kosovo and later to publish my journal. Special thanks go to Gene Lyons and Joyce Castleberry, my readers, for their editorial suggestions. I am indebted to Gene for more than help with the book, however. Twenty-three years ago in Little Rock, Arkansas, Gene and his wife, Diane, arranged a blind date for their neighbor, Paula, with their friend, Ed, who was visiting from California. Gene and Diane, what can I say, except—thank you.

❧

If you would like to help provide educational opportunities for young Kosovars, please send a check or money order to:

SUNY New Paltz Foundation
For the Paula Huntley Kosovar Student Scholarship Fund
State University of New York at New Paltz
75 S. Manheim Boulevard, Suite 9
New Paltz, NY 12561

A portion of the proceeds from this book will be donated to this fund.

For information about other ways to help the people of Kosovo, visit:
www.hemingwaybookclubofkosovo.com.